Hydraulic Lime Mortar

for Stone, Brick and Block Masonry

Hydraulic Lime Mortar

for Stone, Brick and Block Masonry

Geoffrey Allen
Jim Allen
Nick Elton
Michael Farey
Stafford Holmes
Paul Livesey
Mileva Radonjic

DONHEAD

UK LIMES
DTI acronym

First Published 2003 by
Donhead Publishing Ltd
Lower Coombe
Donhead St Mary
Shaftesbury
Dorset
SP7 9LY
www.donhead.com

ISBN 1 873394 64 0

Printed by TJ International, Padstow

IMPORTANT NOTICE
This publication is intended solely for use by professional personnel and qualified tradesman who are competent to evaluate the significance and limitations of the information contained herein, and who will accept total responsibility for the application of the information.

The Foresight Lime Research Team has used all reasonable care to ensure the information herein contained is accurate but no liability can be accepted for any loss or damage arising from any inaccuracy, whether due to their negligence or otherwise.

Contents

Foresight Lime Project Participants

The following persons and organizations have contributed to the research and drafting of this guide:

Mr M. Farey, Hydraulic Lias Limes Ltd, Project Manager
Professor G. Allen, Interface Analysis Centre, Bristol University
Dr J. Allen, Ellis & Moore (Consulting Engineers)
Dr N. Elton, Bristol University (previously with Imery's Minerals Ltd)
Mr S. Holmes, Rodney Melville & Partners, Architects
Mr P. Livesey, Castle Cement Ltd
Dr M. Radonjic, Interface Analysis Centre, Bristol University

Acknowledgements

This publication has resulted from a three-year research programme based at the University of Bristol, 50 per cent funded by the Engineering and Physical Sciences Research Council (EPSRC). The balance of the considerable cost was borne by the team members all of whom with the exception of myself represent a huge range of skills and experience within the UK construction industry and scientific community.

The Interface Analysis Centre of Bristol University, directed by Professor Geoff Allen, provided the research base and Dr Mileva Radonjic undertook the electron microscopy. Dr Jim Allen, from consulting engineers Ellis & Moore, provided a vital engineering component to the team, often helping in the early days to keep the work focused on what was achievable.

Next, Stafford Holmes, the architect and joint author of *Building With Lime*, whose tolerant partners in the practice of Rodney Melville and Partners have learnt to accept his passion. Stafford worked ceaselessly, providing sites for examination as well as access to his huge private database of information.

Arguably the most unlikely member of the team was Paul Livesey who, whatever his official company post, is undeniably Castle Cement's chief scientist. I understand that during the programme his director at Castle Cement asked him 'Paul, I thought we were a cement company, not a lime company?' This question clearly indicates the amount of work Paul and his laboratory staff undertook over the three years. His figures show that over 1,500 separate samples were made and tested on top of the laboratories' normal test programme.

When the research was being planned, English China Clay (ECC) was a member and provided Dr Nick Elton, a very talented member of its research team at Par Moor Laboratories, St Austell. As the programme began, ECC was taken over and shortly afterwards the research department closed making nearly all the staff, including Nick, redundant. We all felt upset for Nick and missed his important input.

The team also owe their thanks to The National Trust and the Church Preservation Trust for their help at Hardwick Hall and Richmond Castle respectively.

As well as providing you, the reader, with the data to use hydraulic lime with a greater understanding, the team had another aim – to push forward the production of UK manufactured hydraulic lime instead of being dependant on imports.

Michael J Farey
April 2003

Preface

Despite successful use over many centuries hydraulic limes were relegated almost to history (along with how to use them) when ordinary Portland cement (OPC) came into widespread use. Now for a whole variety of reasons their benefits, quite rightly, are being reassessed.

So what are hydraulic limes? In this context it means that they can set partially under water, as a result of a chemical reaction. Out of water setting by carbonation will also occur.

Conversely, non-hydraulic limes can only set by carbonation, that is absorbing carbon dioxide from the atmosphere. The proportion of the set attributable to the chemical reaction, as opposed to carbonation will determine each hydraulic lime's characteristics and performance. Furthermore other variations can be introduced by differences in the chemical compounds contained within the limes. Overall, these factors give designers and contractors considerable flexibility in selection of the correct material for the job. The publication of this book along with manufacturers data, should for the first time help in enabling hydraulic limes to be successfully specified and used.

This publication has been produced as a result of research carried out as part of the Engineering and Physical Sciences Research Council (EPSRC)/Department of Trade and Industry Foresight research project on the 'Performance, application and classification of hydraulic limes and pozzolans for the UK construction industry'.

It deals with constituent materials, mix design, mortar properties, workmanship, appearance, strength requirements, and design for durability of the construction relating to hydraulic lime mortar. It is intended that the book should be used in conjunction with other National and International Standards and Codes of Practice relating to the overall construction, function and appearance of the building.

Unless stated otherwise, all references to proportions refer to proportions by volume.

1 *Introduction*

1.1 Mortar – functions

The primary functions of hardened mortar in a construction are:

- To provide an even bed so that the load on the wall is distributed evenly over the whole bearing area of the masonry units;
- To bond the units together and help them resist lateral forces, and
- To seal the joints against the penetration of rain.

1.2 Mortar – properties

In order to achieve the required functions a mortar should be:

- Readily workable to allow the mason to produce satisfactory work at an economic rate;
- Sufficiently resilient when hardened to accommodate minor structural movement, shrinkage or expansion of the construction;
- No stronger than the masonry units to be bonded;
- Durable to suit the purpose of the element of the construction, and
- Aesthetically pleasing in appearance, designed to avoid discord and lack of harmony with the wall finish. For fair-faced work it should enhance, not detract, from the masonry units and be sympathetic to the attractive nature of natural materials, e.g. brick and stone.

The repair of existing buildings requires the mortar to be carefully matched to the original for both function and appearance. A good mortar maintains unity and avoids unsightly contrast. A good match to an existing mortar in performance also reduces the tendency to crack or set up differential movement and weathering characteristics in adjacent areas.

2 *Materials*

2.1 Natural hydraulic lime (NHL)

Natural hydraulic lime is a product produced by burning argillaceous or siliceous limestones followed by reduction to powder by slaking, with or without grinding. All natural hydraulic limes are composed of calcium silicates and aluminates together with calcium hydroxide and some unreacted, inert material. The burning temperature is normally controlled below the clinkering point so that the calcium silicate is predominantly in the di-silicate form (belite) with only trace amounts of the highly reactive tri-silicate (alite) formed in the Portland cement clinkering process. NHLs have the property of being able to set and harden without contact with the air, even under water. When exposed to air, carbonation by reaction with atmospheric carbon dioxide contributes to the hardening process.

The amount of argillaceous and/or siliceous material activated during burning determines the hydraulic reactivity. A new European and British Standard, BS EN 459, specifies the properties and designation as 'HL' and 'NHL' signifying 'hydraulic lime' and 'natural hydraulic lime'. Hydraulic limes are classified according to their reactivity as determined by the development of compressive strength in a standard mortar. The mortar used for their classification has been chosen to give a significant strength with least variability within a limited time, to permit its use as a production quality control parameter. This mortar has the proportions of one part of lime to three parts of a European standard sand, but it should be recognized that these parts are by weight. Also the water content is just sufficient to produce a mortar that can be compacted with heavy vibration. In terms more normally recognized in the construction industry it equates to a mortar of approximately 1:1 by volume with an earth dry consistency of very low workability, i.e. site mixes of these proportions having a water content necessary to achieve adequate workability will not achieve these strengths.

The mortar specified in EN 459 classifies building limes into strength classes of 2, 3.5 or 5 being the minimum compressive strength in N/mm^2 achieved at 28 days in laboratory tests. It is tempting to equate these to the more traditional terms of feebly hydraulic, moderately hydraulic and eminently hydraulic. However, the two classification systems have different bases, the traditional one relating to setting under water whilst the current one relates to strength. It is likely that the compressive strength achieved with modern hydraulic lime mortars is greater than those made with traditional building limes.

2.2 Aggregate

Aggregate in mortar is normally classified as sand or 'fine', for the fraction sized 2.36 mm and below and grit or 'coarse', for that above 2.36 mm. In each case the aggregate should be clean and free from silt and clay which will increase the water demand of the mortar, reduce strength, both compressive and flexural, reduce permeability and increase the risk of cracking in the hardened mortar. Clay might not always show up as fine material since, if dried onto other particles it is not separated by dry sieving. It should be determined by wet separation as described in BS 812. Porous particulates or coarse brick and other dusts acting as pozzolan should be considered as part of the mix aggregate.

Where strength and durability are the priority, aggregate should not contain harmful materials such as iron pyrites, salts, coal or other organic impurities, mica, shale or similar laminated materials, nor flaky or elongated particles in such a form or in sufficient quantity to adversely affect the hardening, strength or durability of the mortar.

If materials other than traditional sand are required in the aggregate for aesthetic or other reasons they will affect the final mortar strength. Separate laboratory testing would be necessary to determine the degree to which they affect the overall performance of the mix.

Historic mortars frequently contain traces of ash, coal and/or charcoal as well as other organic materials such as waterproofing agents and air-entraining proteins. It is possible that these contributed to frost resistance by preventing moisture absorption and hence freezing or by providing porosity allowing sites of stress relief from expansion forces during freezing. These aspects and the mortar requirements to resist frost are discussed further in section 4.5.

The choice of sand and other aggregates for mortar is most important. The aggregate is responsible for the mortar structure, which plays a key role in the development of strength and permeability. Grading curves (Figure 1) show the proportion by mass of the sand retained on standard sieves between 5 mm and 0.075 mm (75 microns) and can be compared with the grading specified for mortar in BS 1200: Type S. The grading curve should show good distribution between the various sizes. Too great a concentration of one or two size(s), although it might conform to the requirements of BS 1200 Type S, will diminish workability, and require the addition of more water to achieve the correct consistency, and can lead to bleeding and staining of the mortar (see section 2.3). A sand with a preponderance of coarse particles will be harsh and difficult to work. European Standard, EN 13139 Aggregates for mortar, gives little helpful guidance when formulating lime mortars.

Examples of well-graded sand and single sized sand are shown in Figure 1. Curves 1a and 1b show the traditional form for comparing gradings with specification ranges. Bar charts 1c and 1d show the distribution between sizes more clearly.

In general the maximum particle size of the sand and aggregate should not exceed one half of the joint width. For applications employing joints of 8 to 12 mm, the maximum size will accord with BS 1200 at 5 mm. In some applications, such as ashlar work with fine joints, it might be necessary to reduce the maximum size to 3 mm, or less, whilst still maintaining good distribution between sizes. Alternatively, where wider joints are used, coarse aggregate of 5 mm and above may be incorporated.

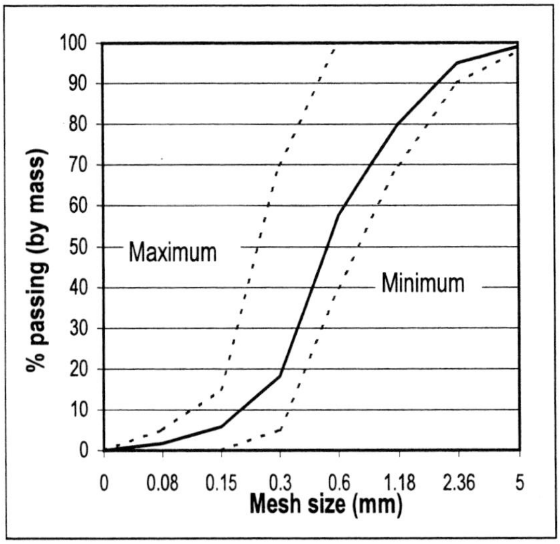

Figure 1a *Example of well-graded sand compared with BS 1200 requirements.*

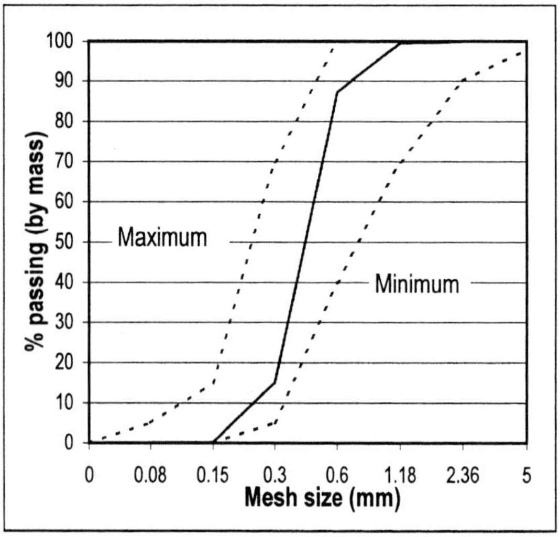

Figure 1b *Example of poorly-graded sand compared with BS 1200 requirements*

The use of coarse aggregate will increase the harshness of the mix so that the amount used should be adjusted to retain workability. Coarse aggregate should be graded and analysed separately using sieves of 6.3 mm, 10 mm and 14 mm as appropriate.

Distribution of sizes in the sand is important in order to achieve close packing in the mortar structure. Even with good distribution there will still be voids between individual particles and these need to be filled with the binder. The space between the sand particles – the

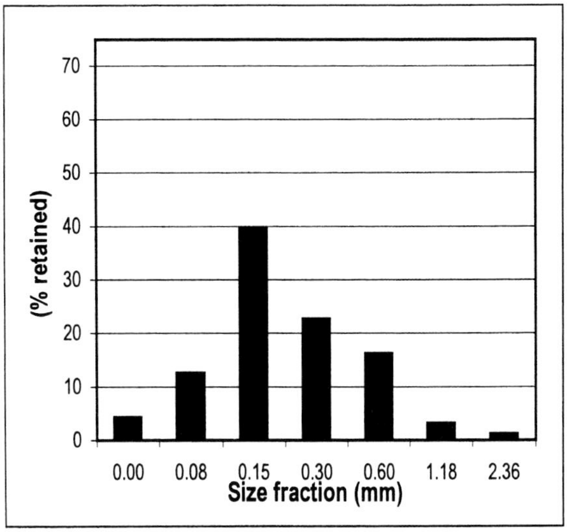

Figure 1c *Example of well-graded sand showing fraction size distribution*

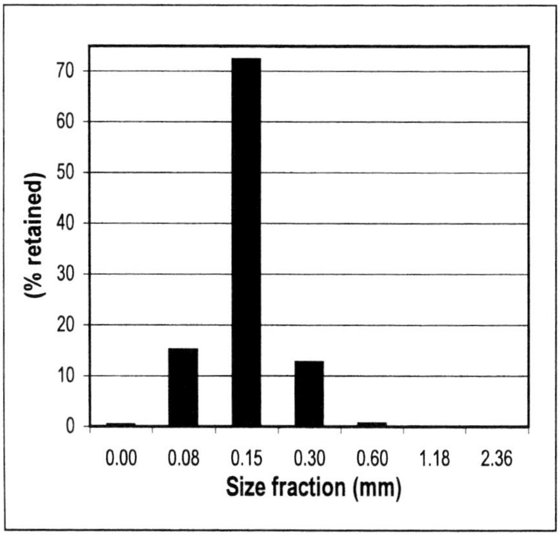

Figure 1d *Example of poorly-graded sand showing fraction size distribution*

voidage – can be measured by checking the quantity of water required to fill the space. The properties of a good mortar must include binder content sufficient to fill this void space. This filling should not be confused with the degree of permeability, which is determined by the characteristic hydration products of the binder.

Whilst the above is 'best practice' it is often more economical to use the material available locally, even though it might require a richer mix, rather than to bring in aggregate from farther afield. This is often the case when matching an existing mortar in an old building. It should be stressed that, although there are desirable properties for good grading, no ideal grading exists, and excellent mortars have been produced with a wide range of aggregate gradings. An important feature of satisfactory aggregate is the continuous uniformity of grading for the whole project so that the characteristics of the mortar do not change with every delivery.

2.3 Water

The quality of water can affect the setting and strength of the mortar. Potable (drinkable) water, or water meeting the requirements of BS EN 1008 should be suitable. Other waters can be used but should not contain suspended solids, which add to the silt content, nor dissolved solids, which might cause staining of the hardened mortar. Dissolved salts can be detrimental to the durability of mortar and organic impurities can affect hardening and durability. Traditional and synthetic organic materials added to improve properties, e.g. air-entraining agents to improve frost resistance, should be tested to ensure they have no deleterious effects.

2.4 Additions

General

Additions are materials added to a mortar to improve the plastic properties or to enhance the hardened properties. They can be inert or possess pozzolanic properties, i.e. when mixed with water and lime they will form hydration products similar to those obtained by the hydration of hydraulic limes. Details of additions, their chemistry, particle size and hydraulicity are set out in Appendix B.

Pozzolans

Pozzolanic materials do not harden in themselves when mixed with water but, when finely ground and in the presence of water, they react at normal ambient temperature with dissolved calcium hydroxide ($Ca(OH)_2$) to form strength-developing calcium silicate and calcium aluminate compounds. These compounds are similar to those formed in the hardening of hydraulic materials. Pozzolans consist essentially of reactive silicon dioxide (SiO_2) and aluminium oxide (Al_2O_3), the remainder being more or less inert consists of iron (Fe_2O_3) and other oxides. They rarely contain significant proportions of reactive calcium oxide or hydroxide.

Natural pozzolans are usually materials of volcanic origin or sedimentary rocks with suitable chemical and mineralogical composition. The term 'pozzolan' is used to denote the generic material whilst 'pozzolana' is retained for traditional material from Pozzuoli in Italy.

Pozzolanic materials need to be correctly prepared, i.e. selected, homogenised, dried, or heat-treated and crushed, depending on their state of production or delivery. Natural pozzolana or artificial pozzolan in the form of fired clay brick or tile, have traditionally been used in mortars to produce or improve hydraulic set and hardened properties. Fine pozzolana should be considered as part of the binder. Coarse pozzolan, often porous, can be used to improve the permeability of the mortar and is then treated as part of the aggregate.

Calcium lime

Calcium lime, or air lime, is produced in various forms: quicklime, dry hydrated lime or lime putty. It has been used as a constituent of mortar from earliest times. The modern material, CL90 according to BS EN 459-1, is a very pure form of calcium hydroxide, ($Ca(OH)_2$), and as such does not contribute directly to the hydraulic activity. It can be used in hydraulic lime mortars to enhance the free lime content, improve the plasticity of leaner hydraulic lime mortars, provide an additional source of lime for reaction with pozzolans and provide an additional source of available lime in the hardened mortar to enhance autogenous healing.

Lime putty

Lime putty is another form of calcium lime supplied as a suspension of lime in water. Because moisture is present it is essential that it is kept in airtight containers and that a layer of water is maintained on the surface of the suspension to prevent carbonation. Prolonged storage of lime putty allows it to dissolve and re-crystallise repeatedly, which results in much finer than normal crystal sizes that enhance its plasticizing ability. In other respects it acts as dry calcium lime although the fine particle size and the suspended solid form increase the water demand of the mortar, thereby reducing hardened strength and increasing the tendency to drying shrinkage. In the Foresight project it was found that more than 10 per cent volume/volume of wet putty to dry natural hydraulic lime class 3.5 significantly reduced mortar strength and durability.

Filler

Filler is fine material incorporated into mortar, generally to improve the properties of the wet mortar. The particle size of filler is usually taken as below 90 microns and can consist of ground limestone, chalk, sand or clay. These materials are advantageous in complementing the grading of sands deficient in fines, where to fill the void structure with hydraulic lime would result in too strong a mortar.

3 Mortar Mix Design

3.1 General

To obtain optimum and consistent performance from any mortar it is essential that the correct constituent proportions are reproduced on site. To achieve this it is necessary to have an accurate system for batching materials. At best this will be by weight. Where this is not possible, an accurate set of volume gauges should be established. Greatest reliability will be achieved using a mixer, sufficiently large to permit full bags of lime to be mixed in a single batch; a sand gauge in the form of a strong bucket or gauge box with a designated number of full buckets and level gauges per mix established; a similar gauge for any other dry constituent; and a water addition sequence as set out in the workmanship section (see section 5). Care should be taken to ensure that sand is neither too dry nor too wet so that the effect of bulking with wetting is limited. Errors as great as 40 per cent by mass can result when batching wet sand. The effect of moisture on the bulk density of sand should be determined when designing the mix.

3.2 Maximum aggregate size

The larger the aggregate particle, the smaller the surface area to be wetted. Thus extending the range of aggregate size above the traditional 5 mm lowers the water content of the mix so that, for a specified workability and richness of mix, the water content is reduced resulting in a reduced tendency to shrink and a general improvement in properties. There are practical limitations to this and as a general guide the maximum size should be no greater than 50 per cent of the mortar joint width. For a traditional 10–12 mm joint the maximum size would be the traditional 5 mm. Fine joints for ashlar work might require a maximum of 3 mm or less, down to buttered joints with no aggregate, and in the case of wider joints for rubble walling, inclusion of aggregate of up to 10 mm would be appropriate.

The type of aggregate suitable for use in sizes greater than 5 mm can be grit from the same source as the sand or, preferably, crushed stone of the same type as the walling unit or, where improved permeability is required, more porous aggregate. The overall aggregate grading should follow the principles of BS 1200 restricting the quantity of each size to ensure even grading of the overall aggregate. Where coarse aggregate is included, this can be achieved by separately checking the fraction above 5 mm for void content and designing to ensure that the volume of the lime/sand mortar fraction is sufficient to fill the void.

The use of coarse aggregate in this form in the mortar should not be confused with galleting, tile slips or pinnings where large fragments are inserted into cavities to give added stability and to avoid excessively thick mortar sections. Such techniques are designed to counter the tendency of large areas of mortar to shrink to a greater extent than the general run of mortar. Excessively thick mortar joints with only fine aggregate can lead to an increased risk of early-age cracking.

3.3 Aggregate grading

Fine aggregate (below 5 mm) should be analysed separately and the choice of this sand grading has already been discussed in section 2.2. In some cases it might be necessary to combine sands to achieve an adequate grading. The void content of the sand should be checked and this should be less than the volume of lime particles in the mix. For mixes incorporating fine pozzolans the volume of the pozzolan particles should be added to that of the lime for comparison with the sand void space. Insufficient binder to fill the void space will result in a harsh mortar with an unnecessarily high water content resulting in lower strength and reduced resistance to frost. Where there is insufficient binder to fill the void space the grading of the sand and the proportion of binder should be reviewed. Selection of binder class, and whether to include pozzolan, gives further options for adjustment of void filling capacity. Pigments or coloured sands and aggregate included to achieve specific colours should be treated as part of the aggregate and included in the grading.

3.4 Binder content

The binder content will be determined by the type of lime used and the class of the mortar required. Table 1 (see page 16) sets out the proportions for the different mortar classes. It gives choices of mortar types to suit a specific class and selection of that most appropriate for available materials, or to meet the sand void space requirements.

3.5 Pozzolan additions

Additions are intended to improve the performance of the mortar or the properties of the plastic mortar. It is customary to consider pozzolans as additions to the batch weights determined for lime and sand, that is, having determined the relative volumes of lime and sand, these should be maintained and the required volume of pozzolan batched in addition (e.g. a mix described as 1:3 + 10%). In practice pozzolans act as partial replacements for both lime and sand. In assessing the performance of pozzolan-modified mixes attention has to be given to any change in the density of the mortar and any constituent of the pozzolan that might affect resistance to chemical agents.

Calcium lime (air lime or dry hydrated lime) is regarded as part of the binder. A convention has been developed in Scandinavia whereby binders incorporating calcium lime are described by their proportions by mass, e.g. 80:20 NHL 5:CL90 would consist of 80% by mass of hydraulic lime and 20% by mass of calcium lime. Details of these are set out in Appendix B.

4 Mortar Properties

4.1 General

The mortar should be readily workable to allow the mason to produce satisfactory work at an economic rate. A good mortar will hang on the trowel and spread easily. It should not readily lose water and stiffen when brought into contact with masonry units having moderate suction (masonry units with 7%–12% absorption, normally exhibit moderate suction to hydraulic lime mortars, when tested in accordance with BS 3921: Appendix E). When high suction masonry is being used it is necessary to limit the suction by pre-wetting the units, taking care to ensure there is no free water on the surface when the mortar is applied. When low suction masonry is being used it is necessary to design the mortar to ensure good adhesion, generally by increasing fines content and/or reducing water content and/or increasing the free lime content. Such properties will help to develop a good bond between bricks and mortar and lessen the risk of water penetration through the finished wall. Care and experience is required to ensure correct mix design for specific applications.

4.2 Mortar plastic properties

A guide to the plastic properties of typical mortars is set out in Table 1. It provides guidance for design and conformity testing of mortars. The values in Table 1 for mix proportions by mass, water/lime ratio, hydraulic lime content and plastic density are for guidance and will vary depending on the sand source, water demand to achieve required workability, and air content of the plastic mortar. It is necessary to establish values for the combination, and factors applicable to individual mortars.

Hydraulic lime class	Mix proportions by volume (lime:sand)	Mix proportions by mass (lime:sand)	Water/Lime ratio[1]	Hydraulic lime content (kg/m^3)	Plastic density (kg/m^3)
NHL 2	1:2	1:6	1.00	260	2045
	1:2.5	1:7.5	1.35	210	2035
	1:3	1:9	1.45	180	2035
NHL 3.5	1:1	1:2.5	0.70	455	1930
	1:1.5	1:4	0.85	330	1870
	1:2	1:5	1.00	270	1910
	1:2.5	1:6	1.10	245	1945
	1:3	1:7.5	1.40	190	1885
	1:4	1:10	1.75	150	1900
	1:6	1:15	2.80	100	1900
NHL 5	1:2	1:4	0.65	375	2105
	1:3	1:6	1.00	265	2090
	1:4	1:8	1.40	200	2110

Table 1 *Typical proportions and properties of mortars tested in the Foresight project.*

Notes 1. Mortar water content was adjusted to achieve workability typical of that used on site.

4.3 Strength

Compressive strength

The strength of mortar will depend upon its constituents, particularly the class of lime and whether pozzolan is included, the proportions, the water content, its age, and the temperature and relative humidity at which it has matured. Figure 2 sets out the strength development of NHL 3.5 hydraulic lime mortar as sampled in accordance with Appendix A, according to mix proportions and age cured at 20°C.

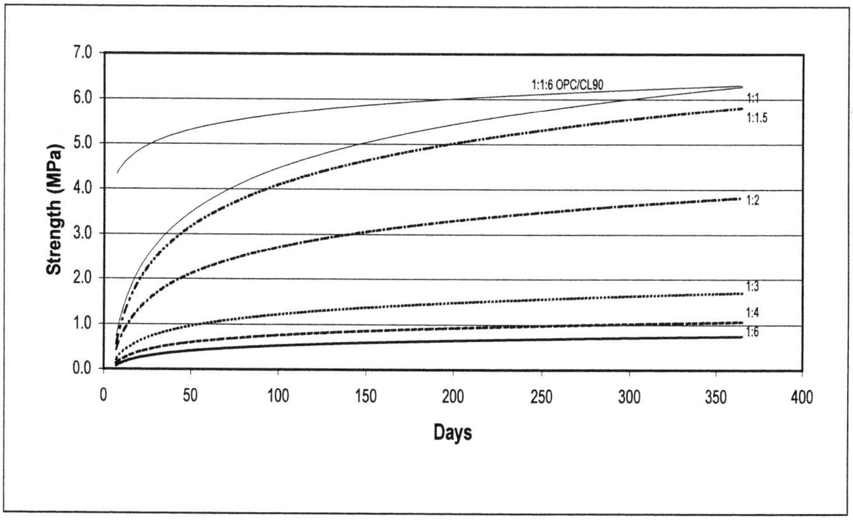

Figure 2 *Strength development of NHL 3.5 hydraulic lime mortars by mix proportions.*

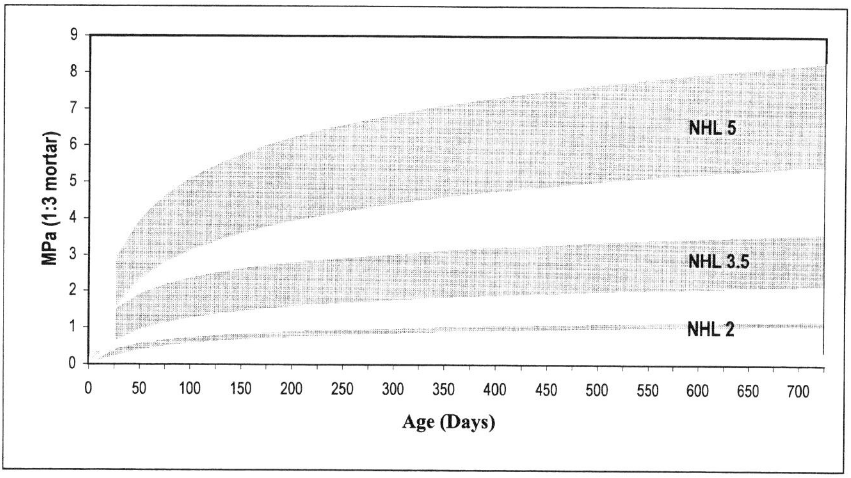

Figure 3 *Strength development of natural hydraulic lime mortars by lime strength class.*

Figure 3 sets out the strength development for a range of 1:3 mortars containing natural hydraulic limes of the three strength classes available in the UK at the time of the Foresight project. It can be seen that for the most part the standard classification according to strength is mirrored in their relative performance in typical mortars.

Lime content

Strength, of a given hydraulic lime, is controlled by the hydraulic lime content of the mix. Figure 4 shows a typical relationship between hydraulic lime content and strength.

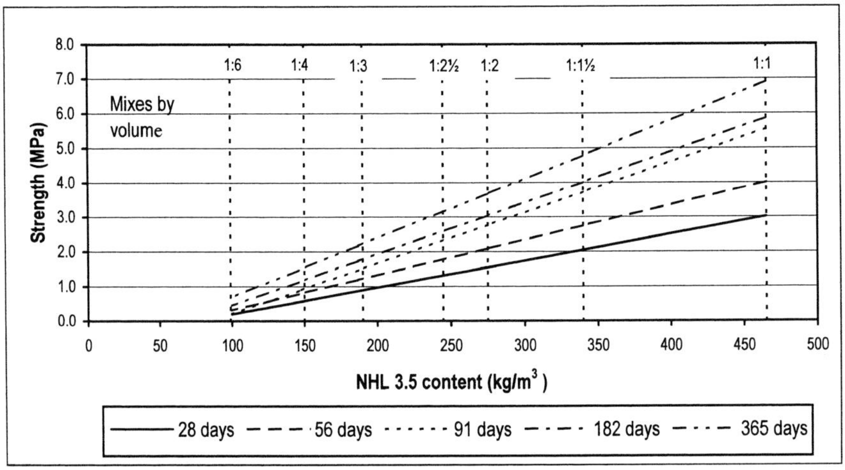

Figure 4 *Relationship between NHL 3.5 lime content and compressive strength.*

Water/lime ratio

Strength, for a given hydraulic lime and lime content, is controlled by the water/lime ratio of the mix. Figure 5 shows a typical relationship between water/lime ratio and strength.

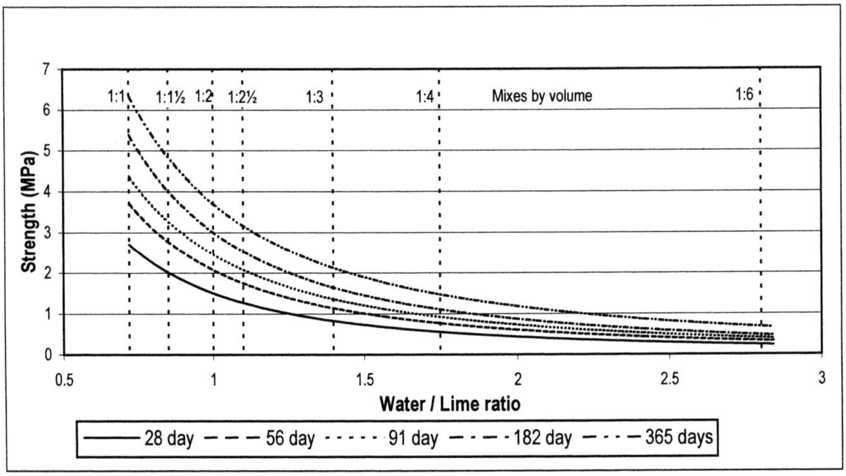

Figure 5 *Relationship between water/lime ratio and strength.*

Flexural strength

Flexural strength is also a significant property of hydraulic lime mortars. Table 2 sets out the relationship between flexural and compressive strengths for hydraulic lime class 3.5 mortars and for a Portland cement:lime mortar. A reduction in flexural strength as a percentage of the compressive strength indicates reduced plasticity and increased brittleness. Figure 6 shows a typical relationship between flexural strength and the water/lime ratio for hydraulic lime class 3.5 mortar.

Age (days)	Flexural strength (as % of compressive strength) (mix proportions by volume)				
	1:1 NHL 3.5: sand	1:1.5 NHL 3.5: sand	1:2 NHL 3.5: sand	1:3 NHL 3.5: sand	1:1:6 PC:CL90: sand
7	76	78	80	80	30
14	52	54	64	70	31
28	47	49	56	67	32
56	44	46	53	65	33
91	42	45	51	64	33
182	40	44	50	61	34
365	39	43	49	55	34

Table 2 *Relationship between flexural and compressive strengths of mortars.*

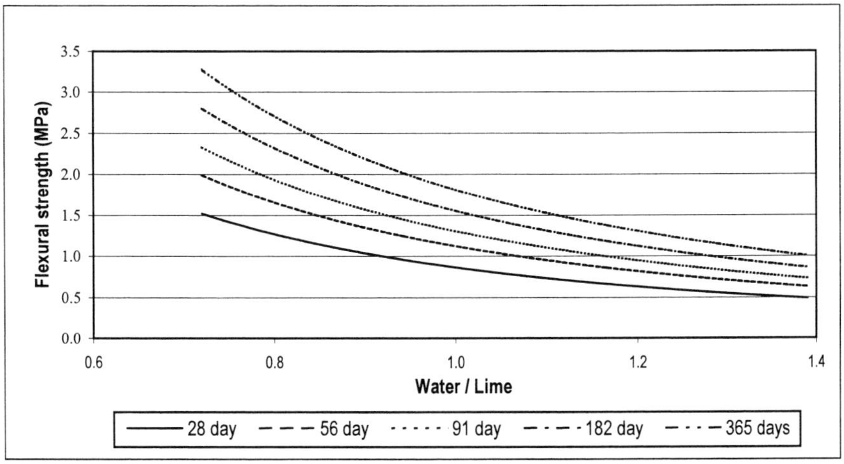

Figure 6 *Flexural strength and water/lime ratio relationship.*

Temperature effects

Strength, for a given hydraulic lime, lime content and water:lime ratio, is affected by the temperature at which the mix is cured. Figure 7 shows a typical relationship between temperature and compressive strength. Table 3 sets out the relative maturities for mortars cured at the different temperatures.

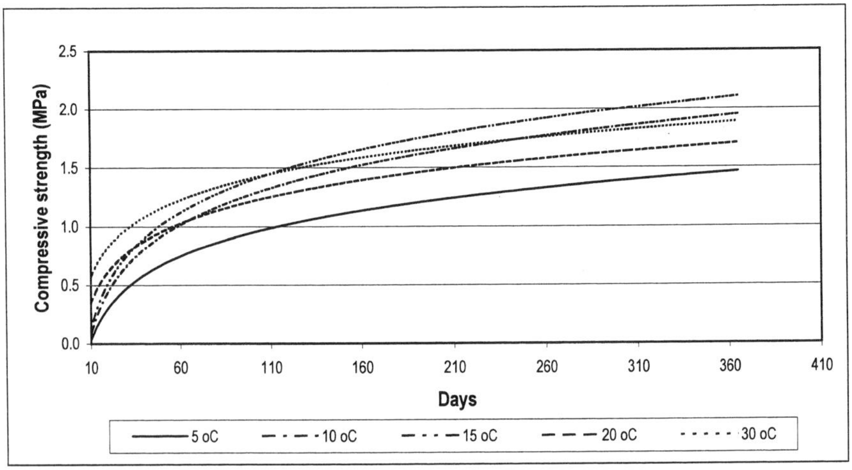

Figure 7 *Strength development of mortar with temperature. The temperature relates to that during the first 28 days, thereafter cured at 20°C.*

Age (days)	Compressive strength (% of 20°C strength)				
	@ 5°C	@ 10°C	@ 15°C	@ 20°C	@ 30°C
28	40	65	80	100	145
56	65	90	100	100	125
91	75	100	110	100	120
182	85	110	120	100	115
365	90	120	130	100	110

Table 3 *Temperature effect on maturity for 1:3 (by volume) NHL 3.5:sand mortars.*

4.4 Permeability

Lime mortars possess the basic characteristic of high permeability, particularly to vapour. The measurement of vapour permeability in fragile specimens such as hydraulic lime mortars is outside the scope of the current Foresight project and such methods are more appropriate to the research environment. However, water permeability can be determined relatively simply and provides a comparator for the general permeability characteristics of the various mortars. The test method employed was that of capillarity whereby a 40 mm x 40 mm x 160 mm prism of mortar, matured for 90 days and pre-conditioned by exposure to laboratory air at 60 per cent relative humidity / 20°C for seven days, was stood on the 40 mm x 40 mm end and immersed in 10 mm of water for 24 hours. The capillary rise measured by the water absorption level gave a measure of permeability. The method is also applicable to masonry units. Results are set out in Table 4.

Category (mm rise @ 6 hours)	**Mortars**
Very high (126–150)	NHL 2 1:3 NHL 3.5 1:4 NHL 3.5 1:6 NHL 3.5 1:3 + 10% putty NHL 3.5 1:3 + 30% CL90 CL90 mortars CL90 +30% metakaolin (also Ketton freestone)
High (101–125)	NHL 2 1:2 NHL 3.5 1:3 + 10% CL90 NHL 3.5 1:3 + 5% putty
Moderate (76–100)	NHL 3.5 1:2½ NHL 3.5 1:3 NHL 3.5 1:3 + brickdust NHL 5 1:4 (also OPC:CL90 1:3:12, Ancaster stone and Portland stone)
Low (51–75)	NHL 3.5 1:1 NHL 3.5 1:1½ NHL 3.5 1:2 NHL 3.5 1:3 + natural pozzolana NHL 3.5 1:3 + 50% CL90 NHL 3.5 1:3 + slag, fly ash, metakaolin, microsilica NHL 5 1:3 (also OPC:CL90 1:2:9 and Cadeby stone)
Very low (<51)	NHL 5 1:2 (also OPC:CL90 1:1:6, Masonry cement 1:4, Clipsham stone and Stokeground stone)

Table 4 *Capillary rise for mortars and natural stones.*

Note that the permeability of some stones will vary with location and level in the quarry.

4.5 Frost resistance

Resistance of the various mortars to cycles of freezing at -5°C and thawing at 20°C is set out in Table 5. The method used was to cure specimens at 20°C and 90+% RH to 91 days; they were then immersed in mains water, towelled dry to SSD (Saturated Surface Dry) and weighed; frozen for at least six hours with tooled face uppermost and other faces wrapped in insulation; thawed in air for at least twelve hours; weighed and examined for cracks; and re-immersed in water for at least six hours. Results are the cycles to failure, i.e. when specimens broke. Mature mortars of hydraulic lime class 3.5 in proportions of 1:2½ to 1:1½ are considered to exhibit high frost resistance.

Category	Mortar (proportions by volume)
Very high (>50 cycles)	NHL 3.5 1:2 NHL 5 1:2 NHL 5 1:3 (also OPC:CL90 1:1:6 and Masonry cement 1:4)
High (26–50 cycles)	NHL 3.5 1:2½ NHL 3.5 1:1½ NHL 5 1:4 (also OPC:CL90 1:2:9)
Moderate (10–25 cycles)	NHL 3.5 1:1 NHL 3.5 1:3 NHL 3.5 1:4
Low (<10 cycles)	NHL 3.5 1:6 NHL 2 1:2 NHL 2 1:3 (also CL90 mortars)

Table 5 *Resistance to freezing/thawing cycles.*

4.6 Sulfate resistance

Results of tests on resistance to sulfate solution (2% potassium sulfate) are set out in Table 6. The method used was to cure specimens at 20°C and 90+% RH to 91 days; they were then immersed in potassium sulfate solution (2% SO_3) with tooled face uppermost; allowed to dry at 20°C, 65% RH twice weekly; weighed and examined for cracks; and re-immersed. Results are the cycles to failure, i.e. when specimens

Category	Mortars
Very high (>50 cycles)	NHL 3.5 1:1 NHL 3.5 1:1½ NHL 3.5 1:2 NHL 3.5 1:2½ NHL 3.5 1:3 NHL 3.5 1:4 NHL 5 1:2 NHL 5 1:3 NHL 5 1:4 (also CL90 mortars, OPC:CL90 1:1:6 and Sulfate-resisting masonry cement 1:4)
High (26–50 cycles)	NHL 2 1:2 NHL 2 1:3 (also OPC:CL90 1:2:9)
Moderate (10–25 cycles)	NHL 3.5 1:6
Low (<10 cycles)	OPC:plasticizer mortars

Table 6 *Resistance to sulfate exposure.*

broke. All natural hydraulic limes exhibit good sulfate resistance with no deterioration observed regarding either alumina or sulfate content. As comparison the 1:1:6 OPC:CL90:sand mix was confirmed by the Building Research Establishment as meeting their sulfate-resisting mortar requirements.

4.7. Resistance to freezing and thawing in sulfates

Table 7 sets out the results of tests on resistance to the combined effect of sulfate and frost. The method used was to cure specimens at 20°C and 90+% RH to 91 days; they were then immersed in potassium sulfate solution (2% SO_3) with tooled face uppermost; frozen at -5°C for at least six hours with tooled face uppermost and all other faces wrapped in insulation; thawed in air for at least twelve hours; weighed and examined for cracks; and re-immersed. Results are the number of cycles to failure, i.e. when specimens broke. Hydraulic lime class 3.5 mature mortars of 1:2½ to 1:1½ are considered to exhibit high resistance to frost in sulfate conditions.

Category	Mortars
Very high (>50 cycles)	NHL 5 1:2 (also OPC:CL90 1:1:6 and Sulfate-resisting masonry cement 1:4)
High (26–50 cycles)	NHL 3.5 1:1½ NHL 3.5 1:2 NHL 3.5 1:2½ NHL 5 1:3 NHL 5 1:4 (also OPC:CL90 1:2:9)
Moderate (10–25 cycles)	NHL 3.5 1:1 NHL 3.5 1:3 NHL 3.5 1:4
Low (<10 cycles)	NHL 3.5 1:6 NHL 2 1:2 NHL 2 1:3 NHL 3.5 1:3 + metakaolin (also CL90 mortars)

Table 7 *Resistance to freezing/thawing cycles in sulfate conditions.*

4.8 Carbonation

Carbonation can benefit hydraulic lime mortars in that it improves the hardening process. Table 8 sets out the results of tests on lime mortars exposed to air at 20°C in high (>90%) relative humidity conditions. The more permeable mortars carbonate quickest. Textured surfaces encourage carbonation to a greater depth and at a faster rate than smooth or heavily worked finishes. The incorporation of porous particulates and air-entraining admixtures also assists in the carbonation process. The rate of carbonation depends on the ambient conditions. Specimens carbonate most quickly in damp but not saturated conditions, specimens in dry or saturated conditions carbonate slowly, if at all. Results are therefore comparative and absolute rates cannot be ascribed to them.

Category	Mortars
Very high	CL90 mortars
High	NHL 2 1:2 NHL 2 1:3 NHL 3.5 1:4 NHL 3.5 1:6 CL90 +10% metakaolin
Moderate	NHL 3.5 1:2½ NHL 3.5 1:3 NHL 3.5 1:3 + brickdust, natural pozzolana NHL 5 1:4 CL90 + 30% metakaolin
Low	NHL 3.5 1:1 NHL 3.5 1:1½ NHL 3.5 1:2 NHL 3.5 1:3 + 10% putty NHL 3.5 1:3 + 50% CL90 NHL 3.5 1:3 + slag, fly ash, metakaolin, microsilica NHL 5 1:2 NHL 5 1:3
Very low	(OPC:CL90 1:1:6 and 1:2:9 and Masonry cement 1:4)

Table 8 *Carbonation rates for mortars exposed to ambient air at 20°C / 90% RH.*

5 *Workmanship*

5.1 Storage of materials

Lime, pozzolans and other bagged materials should be kept on site on a raised floor in a dry store until required. They should be stacked in such a way as to permit use in rotation with each delivery kept separate. The lime from opened bags should be used the same day. The lime from bags damaged, or left open for more than one day should not be used, as binding properties deteriorate with the absorption of carbon dioxide and moisture from the air.

Aggregates and sands should be stored in separate stockpiles on hard clean bases that permit free drainage. Avoid intermixing and contamination from other building materials, debris or other deleterious material. Cover to avoid undue wetting or drying out and check moisture content with each delivery.

Water supply should be arranged such that a convenient tap to dispense mains water is available, an adequate hose length is fitted, or a tank of adequate size and having a convenient tap should be provided. Water heating facilities may be an advantage if work is to continue during cold weather, although working in ambient temperature below 5°C is not recommended when there is a risk of frost.

5.2 Batching

Although the principles of batching have been addressed in section 3 it is always wise to emphasize them since they are so important for achieving optimum and consistent performance from any mortar.

It is essential that the correct constituent proportions are reproduced on site. To achieve this it is necessary to have an accurate system for batching materials. At best this will be by weight. Where this is not possible an accurate set of volume gauges should be established. Greatest reliability will be achieved using a mixer, sufficiently large to permit full bags of lime to be mixed in a single batch; a sand gauge in the form of a strong bucket or gauge boxes with a designated number of full buckets or gauges per mix established; a similar gauge for any other dry constituent; and a water addition sequence as set out in section 5.3. Care should be taken to ensure that sand is neither too dry nor too wet so that the effect of bulking with wetting is limited. The effect of bulking can result in errors of up to 40 per cent when batching wet sand.

5.3 Mixing

The purpose of mixing is to achieve even dispersion of the constituents throughout each batch produced. Lime in particular, because of its very fine particle size, tends to coalesce into bunches of individual grains which, although quite fine themselves, do not permit full wetting of the mix and often require the addition of too much water to achieve the correct workability.

A wide range of mechanical mixers with varying efficiencies can be used. These range from custom-made roller pan mixers, through 'paddle' mixers, pan mixers and screed mixers, to the least efficient, but most often encountered, tilting drum mixer. All can produce good quality mortar providing that close attention is paid to the sequence and rate of addition, the duration of mixing and the rate of water addition. It should be borne in mind that the purpose is to achieve a fully dispersed mix, having the required workability with the minimum addition of water. In order to maintain a well-graded sand/aggregate size the rollers of a roller pan mixer must be set at the appropriate distance off the base to avoid crushing the largest size of aggregate specified.

The principle of mixing is to achieve a good dispersion of lime and other constituents with the 'dry' sand before addition of the mix water. This will ensure that the abrasive nature of the sand assists in breaking down the agglomerated lime particles. The sand should be moist or damp to reduce the amount of lime dust becoming airborne, which can be substantial. This is best achieved by adding proportions of the sand followed by proportions of the lime, allowing a degree of mixing between each part-batch of materials. With a less efficient mixer this can take ten minutes whilst a more efficient mixer will take only five minutes. Once the 'dry' mix is fully dispersed water should be added slowly allowing time for this to become fully dispersed before the final adjustment is made to achieve the required workability. If the site demand for mortar is such that this process is too slow, rather than reduce the essential mixing time, an additional mixer should be provided.

Alternative mixing sequences whereby lime is first mixed with part of the water may be considered, in order to minimize dusting. In this case mixing time may have to be extended to achieve full dispersion and avoid 'balling up' with aggregate particles.

Mixers should not be left rotating indefinitely, so that if the fully mixed mortar is not immediately required the mixer should be stopped and then run for a short time to re-mix the mortar before finally discharging the batch. Alternatively the mortar can be turned out into a skip where it should be kept covered to retain moisture before finally re-mixing within the permitted time (see section 5.5) prior to use.

5.4 Masonry suction

Suction of water from the mortar into the masonry units assists bonding between the two. It contributes to the early stiffening of mortar and stability of the construction. It carries the finer particles, particularly the lime paste, into small voids in the masonry thereby improving the bond.

Masonry units with high suction can absorb so much water that the mortar loses workability rapidly preventing efficient spreading and adjustment of line and level. In such circumstances the masonry units should be pre-wetted on both upper and lower faces. It is preferable to do this well before placing the masonry units to allow time for surface water to be absorbed. The masonry must neither be over-wetted, preventing suction from the mortar, nor have free water on its surface, which can cause slippage on the mortar bed and staining on the finished surface. Masonry units should not be wetted where there is a risk of frost.

5.5 Reworking

Natural hydraulic lime mortars with class 2 and 3.5 limes can generally be re-worked, or 'knocked-up', for up to 24 hours. This time will be shorter for mortars with eminently hydraulic, class 5 natural hydraulic lime, or other stronger mortars incorporating highly active pozzolans. During standing, the water will be acting on any remaining lime agglomerates to disperse them, resulting in improved workability. At the same time the calcium aluminates and silicates will be starting to hydrate, thereby consuming some of the water, with a subsequent loss of workability. These actions should approximately balance each other so that it should be possible to re-work the mortar to the required workability with the minimum of added water. ***If the mix requires significant addition of water it has reacted too far to be useable and should be rejected.*** Mortars intending to be reworked should be covered and protected from environmental influences to keep water loss to a minimum.

5.6 Protection

Protection should be considered for all mortar work after placing. Protection needs to guard against extremes of temperature and moisture, including rainfall and drying winds. Occasionally the weather will be sufficiently mild and humid that protection is not necessary. As this is the exception, provision and procedures should be established so that mortar can always be protected in the early stages after placing. The degree of protection and the time will depend on ambient conditions.

Work should not be carried out if the temperature is below 5°C. Where it is anticipated that the temperature during the first few days might fall to 5°C, or lower, the structure should be protected with damp hessian to preserve the moisture and with sufficient cover, using bubble wrap or insulating material, to protect the structure itself and the mortar against frost. Added precautions may be necessary, possibly including some form of heating, to protect finished work during prolonged periods of freezing temperatures.

Work should not be carried out in direct sunlight, especially in high temperatures, but if this is unavoidable it should be covered as soon as possible with damp hessian to maintain moisture and then with additional cover to prevent the hessian drying out. For best results the moist conditions should be maintained, whilst also allowing air movement over the mortar, for as long as is practicable.

6 Design for Strength

6.1 General

The construction should be designed to have inherent stability and resistance to the forces imposed upon it. These forces might arise from loads imposed, or potential for imposition, wind pressures, impact and other lateral forces and the weight of the construction itself. Strength of brickwork can be affected by the presence of frogs, which should be laid with the larger frog uppermost, filled with mortar where maximum strength is required. The effect on strength is reduced when units with a single frog are laid with the frog down. Consideration should be given to the increase in load, in proportion to developing mortar strength with time as the construction proceeds.

Mortar strength is rarely a limiting factor in the design process, however, the selection of masonry unit and mortar for durability (see section 7) will invariably require a greater type of strength than is directly necessary for resistance to imposed forces.

Potential for cracking in masonry units increases the risk of failure and is affected to a significant degree by the characteristics of the bedding mortar. The choice of mortars should take into account the characteristics of both mortar and masonry thus helping to relieve high stresses, which might otherwise crack the masonry units. It is essential that the strength of the mortar should not exceed that of the masonry unit to be bonded.

6.2 Mortar strength

The selection of the right type of mortar for any particular purpose is of great importance. Its strengths and durability should be based on the recommendations for exposure classification in Table 9 (page 36), according to the type of construction, position in the building, degree of exposure to wind and rain, possibility of early exposure to frost, and type of unit. Consideration of these factors in relation to Table 9 will lead to selection of one of the mortar designations listed in Table 10 (page 39), but in most cases this will allow a choice between several types of mortar within this designation.

The strength of hydraulic lime mortar as mixed on site is given in Table 10. The compressive strengths given for the mortar designations in Table 9 are lower and for later ages than those quoted in BS 5628: Part 1: Table 1 which are for Portland cement mortars. Hydraulic lime mortars develop strength over a longer period and have a greater flexural to compressive strength ratio than do Portland cement mortars (see Table 2, page 19). Consequently their durability and resistance to cracking is greater in relation to compressive strength.

Actual mortar in service is affected by a variable amount of reduction in water content resulting from suction of the masonry. Increased strength due to the age of the mortar should be considered in relation to the strength required during construction and a guide to development of strength over time is given in Figure 3 (page 17). Consideration should also be given to the ambient conditions during construction, particularly temperature, and a guide to the effect of temperature on strength development is given in Figure 7 (page 20).

7 Mortar Selection for Durability

7.1 General

The exposure classification (see Table 9) will be a guide to the most desirable types of masonry unit for a construction and the mortar specification should be determined to match the masonry unit and environmental requirements.

7.2 Resistance to wind and rain

The durability of a mortar and the behaviour of a building in its ability to exclude wind and rain will depend to some extent on its degree of exposure to the elements. This degree of exposure can be judged by the use of the 'driving rain index'. Details appear in the *Building Research Establishment Digest 127* and BS 8104 Code of Practice for assessing exposure of walls to wind driven rain. Consideration of the location by reference to maps will help grade conditions as being sheltered, moderate or severe. Attention should also be paid to particular situations such as whether buildings are excessively high, or exposed. Local conditions which might affect overall grading because of a particular micro-climate must also be considered when deciding exposure grading.

Building element of stone, brick or blockwork[1,2] exposure condition		Proposed range of mortar durability classes for building element[3,4]
Inner leaf of cavity wall and internal walls		1–2
Backing to external solid walls		2–4
External walls including outer leaf of cavity walls in sheltered and moderate locations	Unrendered	1–4
	Rendered[5]	3–4
External walls as facing to solid construction		2–7
Work below or near ground level	Below dpc but no more than 150 mm above finished ground level	5–7
	Below ground or above ground not within 150 mm of ground level[5]	5–7
Sills and cornices		5–8
External free-standing walls excluding capping or coping		5–7
Parapets (excluding capping or coping)	Rendered[5]	5–8
	Unrendered	5–8
Copings, cappings and plinths		5–9
Chimneys and finials[5]		6–9
Retaining walls[5]		6–10
Sewer-bed walls and other unlined walls intended for water retention externally[5]		8–10
Embankment walls, culverts, sluices and engineering work normally below water[5]		9–10

Table 9 *Proposed range of mortar durability for varying building exposure conditions. This is a general guide only, each situation will need to be considered individually on its own merits due to the number of variables and possible permutations of these.*

Notes

1. General guide to classification. Selection of mortar should take into account any structural requirements, the type of construction including that of the masonry units, position in the building, degree of exposure and general properties of the mortar. (See BS 5628: Part 3: 2001, Table 13)
2. Where units have inadvertently become wet, and freezing is likely to occur during or soon after construction, precautions outlined in sections 5.4 and 5.6 should be adopted.
3. When freezing may occur during construction, increase mortar durability class by at least one and adopt the precautions outlined in section 5.6. However, in certain circumstances this procedure may not prevent damage.
4. Mortar durability scale: 1 = minimum exposure; 10 = maximum exposure within the building (see Table 10). Thereafter the durability scale value should be adjusted to take account of the environmental exposure resulting from e.g. prevailing wind, coastal position, hill-side position, sheltered position, etc.
5. Consideration should be given to sulfate resisting mortars (see sections 7.3 and 7.4) where relevant to site conditions.

Table 9 also takes into account the location of the element within the structure and the need for higher classification for exposed applications such as chimneys, parapets, copings, etc.

In the case of old buildings masonry units suitable for the more severe exposure conditions were not always available. Care must be taken therefore to select the appropriate mortar, which is sufficiently durable but no stronger than the adjacent masonry. This is a difficult balance to achieve and additional testing of sample mortars might be necessary. Less durable surfaces may be protected by lime render, which was traditional practice in the past.

7.3 Resistance to frost

The exposure conditions will also indicate the degree of risk of freezing at the structure site. The situation within the structure will indicate the classification of mortar for resistance to this frost risk (see sections 4.5 and 4.7). When using Table 9 in relation to equivalent strength mortars care should be taken to ensure that there is also equivalent resistance to frost.

7.4 Resistance to sulfates

Mortar is subjected to sulfates in various forms. They can be present in the masonry units themselves, they can come from the ground where masonry is in contact with the ground or subjected to moisture movement from the ground through the structure, or can arise in elements such as chimneys exposed to sulfurous gases or airborne gases in a polluted atmosphere. The results set out in Table 6 (page 23) will provide guidance on the selection of appropriate mortar.

7.5 Resistance to sulfate and freezing conditions

External masonry units exposed to freezing conditions might also be subjected to sulfate attack by the routes given above. Table 7 (page 24) provides guidance on selection of appropriate mortars for these conditions.

7.6 Carbonation

Carbonation is beneficial for hydraulic lime mortars in that it increases the hardening process. The more permeable mortars carbonate the quickest. The chemical reaction between lime and carbon dioxide involves the carbon dioxide dissolving in water to form carbonic acid, which then reacts with dissolved lime to form calcium carbonate. Calcium carbonate has low solubility in water and when this threshold is exceeded the calcium carbonate precipitates as crystals, generally of the calcite form. Mortars that are permanently dry will not carbonate. Equally, mortars that continually have a surface layer of water will carbonate only slowly since the surface layer quickly becomes saturated, preventing absorption of carbon dioxide into the body of the mortar. Incorporation of porous particulates or air-entraining admixtures can accelerate the carbonation process.

Mortar designation (hydraulic lime mortar)	NHL 2 lime:sand (vol:vol)[1]	NHL 3.5 lime:sand (vol:vol)[1]	NHL 5 lime:sand (vol:vol)[1]	Mean compressive strength (MPa @ 91 days)[2]	Mortar durability class[3]
HLM 5[4]	–	1:1	1:2	5.0	9–10
HLM 3.5	–	1:1½	1:3	3.5	7–8
HLM 2.5[4]	–	1:2	1:4	2.5	5–6
HLM 1[4]	1:2	1:3	–	1.0	3–4
HLM 0.5	1:3	1:4	–	0.5	1–2

Table 10 *Equivalent hydraulic lime mortar mixes (HLM).*

Notes

1. The proportions in Table 10 are proportions by volume. For proportions by mass see Table 1.
2. Compressive strength of mortar sampled from site and cured and tested according to the scheme set out in Appendix A.
3. Mortar durability class according to Table 9.
4. HLM mortar classes @ 91 days corresponding to MC 28 day classes of BS EN 998-2.

8 Evaluation of Conformity

8.1 General

In any system for evaluation of conformity the specification should form the basis of assessment. A clear and unambiguous statement detailing the works, materials, production and system of assessment is fundamental. The amount of detail and the degree of verification testing requires careful thought to ensure it is proportionate to the importance of the works. In its simplest it might be sufficient to require the use of materials conforming to a standard: visual inspection for cleanliness on receipt, general description of mixes by volume, use of adequate batching gauges, ensuring adequate workability, keeping daily temperature records during winter working and protecting the completed works. More elaborate works might involve the employment of independent quality inspection contractors to monitor every fine detail. Principles for a quality system are set out in BS EN ISO 9002.

8.2 The specification

In drafting the specification consider all details relevant to:

- The materials permitted to be used;
- The mix(es) to be used;
- Any special workmanship requirements;

- Control of documents and data;
- Quality control tests required;
- Conformity assessment tests required;
- Reporting procedures;
- Procedures in the event of non-conformity, and
- Quality of the finished work, both physical and aesthetic.

The detail of the specification should be in proportion to the importance of the works.

8.3 Responsibilities

The contractor and specifier will need to define and set out in the contract the responsible persons who manage, perform and verify work affecting quality, their authority and interrelationships.

Contractors need to ensure that the responsible person has had adequate training and has the authority to:

- Initiate action to prevent occurrence of non-conformities;
- Maintain records relating to the specification, materials and mixes;
- Identify and monitor special workmanship requirements;
- Control further progress until any deficiency has been corrected;
- Liaise with the specifier regarding necessary notifications and reports.

The specifier should ensure that the responsible person has had adequate training and has the authority to:

- Establish with the contractor the arrangements for conformity assessment;
- Confirm that the specification is satisfied;
- Agree with the contractor any arrangements to resolve non-conformities;
- Monitor that corrective measures have been carried out; and
- On conclusion of the works certify that it has been completed in accordance with the specification.

8.4 Materials

Where necessary, the contract documents will detail the materials to be used, their purchasing specifications and approved suppliers. The contractor will need to maintain records of orders, deliveries and any inspections and tests on receipt to ensure the quality of the purchased materials. It is good practice for contractors to clearly set out procedures to ensure satisfactory protection, stock rotation and release of materials.

8.5 Approved mix(es)

The contractor should maintain documented procedures defining:

- Details of the specified mix(es) and their point(s) of application in the structure;
- Production equipment and services to be used;
- Batching equipment;
- Quality control procedures; and
- Maintenance procedures.

8.6 Workmanship requirements

Contractors are responsible for submitting and maintaining documented procedures defining as appropriate:

- Qualifications and appropriate experience of staff;
- Any special requirements for the storage of materials prior to issue to site;
- Any special requirements for the storage of materials on site;
- Batching equipment, identification and verification;
- Mixing procedures including any approvals for 'knocking up';
- Measures to control suction of masonry units; and
- Measures for the protection of completed work.

8.7 Testing for assessment of conformity

It is recommended that contract documents detail under what circumstances and by what means tests should be applied to assess conformity of the works with the specification. They should set out:

- Responsibilities for initiating and carrying out testing;
- Frequency of testing;
- Sampling to be carried out and the sampling procedures;
- Tests to verify the quality of materials on receipt;
- Tests to verify batch gauges, their identification, condition and that they are used;
- Tests to verify mortar workability, visually, by dropping ball or by flow table;
- Tests to verify mortar properties of plastic density and air content;
- Tests to verify mortar hardened properties including the moulds to be used, the curing to apply, the age at which tests are performed, the tests to be applied and laboratories approved to undertake the testing;
- Test result limits for conformity;
- Reports to be prepared, at what stage(s) and their distribution; and
- Actions in the event of non-conformity.

A specimen scheme for assessment of conformity of site mortar is set out in Appendix A.

9 Craftsman's Best Practice Guide

9.1 General guidance for mixing and use of natural hydraulic limes

To obtain the best performance from lime mortars it is essential that the correct sand and lime to water ratios are used. This will include assessment of the masonry units and the engineering design strengths required for the structure. For local building works where the same sands, stone or bricks are used repeatedly, this may only take a few minutes. The factors that affect the strength of a mortar are:

- The type of sand. Soft sands with fine spherical grains make weak mortars. Sharp sands with angular particles including some 3–4 mm grit produce the strongest mortars.
- The water content. Too much water will decrease the mortar strength by holding the grains apart thus leaving an open structure when dry. This effect can be dramatic.
- The amount of binder. In general, the purpose of the binder is to hold the sand particles together and to fill the voids between the grains of sand.
- The type of binder. The strongest binders are those using Portland cement. The weakest are high calcium lime mortars. In between are the hydraulic limes categorized into three strength classes: HL 2: HL

3.5: HL 5 – prefixing the category with N (i.e. NHL 2 or NHL 3.5) indicates a natural hydraulic lime with no additives.

Storage of lime and aggregate

Hydraulic Limes are supplied as a dry powder in bags. Depending upon the source and strength (NHL 2, 3.5 or 5) the colour may vary from off white, to buff to grey. These materials have a shelf life of around six months unless stored in plastic bags when it may be longer. Bags must be kept in a dry store and once opened should be used the same day. Part-used bags can be kept to the next day provided the top is folded down and the material kept in a dry store.

Sands and aggregates

There are many poor quality sands on the market. For good quality lime work – which is about better building – these soft fine sands, frequently containing clay, are not acceptable for most work. Clean sharp, well-graded sands should be specified. A good supplier should be able to provide a sieve analysis against which the sample sieve analysis on page 56 can be compared.

Aggregate should be covered since if left exposed fines can be washed out and the material as a whole can gradually separate. The result will be to make the aggregate less well graded and this may impair durability of the mortar. Covering the aggregate will also stabilize the water content and make mixing more consistent.

Sand void percentage

If you find a good local sand, which you may use repeatedly, establishing a void percentage is a very worthwhile exercise. It is particularly important to establish this when working with unknown materials. The void percentage in the sand will show how much binder is required in order to fill the voids. Insufficient binder will weaken the material and make it vulnerable to frost damage. The procedure to find the void percentage is as follows:

1. Take a container of known volume (a one or two litre jug or jar is ideal).
2. Take a representative sample of the selected sand and dry it completely in an oven on a tray.

3. Replace it in the container to a level top.
4. Take a measured jug of water and gradually add the water until bubbles stop rising and the water has saturated the sand.
5. The void percentage is then:

$$\frac{\text{volume of water added}}{\text{volume of sand}} \times 100$$

Say, for example, the answer is 33%, then a 1 lime to 3 sand (by volume) will fill the voids.

The water content and the masonry units

The more water remaining in the mortar or render, the weaker will be the final result. However too little water will also prevent the chemical processes taking place and weaken the material. The water absorption of the masonry units has a considerable bearing upon the final strength by altering the amount of water left in mortar.

Bricklayers and masons will normally add sufficient water to obtain adequate workability. However if the tradesmen are not used to mortars with sharp sands it is possible that too much water may be added.

It is strongly recommended that either:

- Manufacturers absorption figures are obtained for the masonry; or
- The following test is carried out:
  1. The brick/stone is oven dried and weighed;
  2. The brick/stone is then placed in bucket of water for two hours and then re-weighed.

Water percentage drawn into the masonry can then be established. Optimum strength is likely to be achieved with the final water content in the mortar also established. Typically this could be around 15% by mass (weight) after suction of water by the masonry using a typical sharp sand of 36% voids.

A simple alternative method of dealing with this is to soak all bricks before use. However, bricks should not be soaked in cold frosty weather, surface damping is adequate.

Mix and technique

A conventional cement mixer can be used, although for larger projects a rollpan or paddle mixer is preferable. These are becoming more readily available as a result of the renewed interest in lime products. The mix will vary over the range indicated in table 1 (page 16), depending upon conditions and location. Measuring of material must always be with a gauging box or bucket. A shovel is not acceptable since quantities are too inconsistent. Paddle mixers are preferable to roller pan mixers as the rollers may crush the aggregate if not set sufficiently clear of the pan.

Lime mortars mixed in drum mixers can be prone to balling and use of particular mixing techniques can reduce this. It is therefore recommended that a small quantity of water is put into the mixer while not rotating and then the appropriate quantity of lime added. When the mixer is switched on the lime should be turned into a wet slurry. The sand is added to the slurry, with more water, and mixed for not less than 15–20 minutes. Alternative mixing sequences, e.g. adding lime and sand before the water, may be used when this does not lead to unduly dusty conditions. Do not overfill the mixer as this will prevent proper mixing.

The mix, to begin with, should appear rather dry but as mixing time increases the mortar will become much 'fattier'. At the end of twenty minutes the final water can be added to obtain the correct workability if required. If too much water is added the risk of shrinkage will increase and the final strength reduced.

Use of air entrainment agent

It is acceptable to use air entrainment agents. More will be required than recommended for cement mortars. Workability will be improved and long-term durability enhanced. Generally, an air entrainment agent will enhance the performance of mortars and renders by increasing frost resistance, improving workability and reducing water damage.

Additional pozzolan

In cold weather and for certain other applications it may be advantageous to add additional pozzolan in order to increase the speed of set and/or increase strength. It is recommended that professional advice is sought or the lime manufacturer or local agent be consulted as to the quantities of these materials to be added since the amount will vary depending upon the type of work being undertaken.

After-care

The mortar must be kept moist for several days after application. The curing time will vary depending on ambient conditions. Remember, water is essential for both carbonation and the hydraulic set; it is important while maintaining the moisture to prevent rapid drying from wind and bright sunlight. Covering the work with damp hessian and keeping this damp is the best procedure.

If there is a risk of frost, hessian covers should again be used. Bubble wrap or other insulating material outside the hessian can also be added for insulation. For more detail on after-care please read section 9.3.

9.2 Techniques for mortars in wall construction and pointing

Mortar strength designation

Mortar designations are contained in BS5628 Part 1, Table 1. For the majority of conventional construction a Type (iv) mortar will be adequate. A compressive strength of 1.5 newtons/mm^2 should be attainable with an NHL 3.5, provided average ambient temperature exceeds 10°C. Below this, the rate of strength build up may slow down work.

For exterior work, when mortar joint size permits, the sand should contain a small proportion of 3–4 mm grit.

Generally a 1:3 NHL 3.5 lime:sand ratio by volume will be sufficiently strong to provide a Type (iv) mortar.

Additional durability requiring a 1:2 mix will be needed for the following areas of building exposure (or NHL 5 or NHL 3.5 1:1½ and/or the addition of pozzolan will be required in more severely exposed locations subject to adjacent masonry strength):

- Chimneys
- Parapets
- Copings
- Splash areas at base of walls
- Below DPC

Mortar mixes will also need to be adjusted to take into account the environmental exposure, i.e. direction of driving rain, wind, frost, coastal or sheltered locations.

In addition, if the structural requirements dictate a Type (iii) mortar strength, preparation and after care become more critical. The following points need highlighting:

- The mortar should be very well mixed – balling must be avoided. Remember air entrainment and consider the use of air entrainment agents. Always measure using a gauging box or bucket.
- Mortar must not be allowed to dry out too quickly. This is especially important with porous masonry, which may require wetting before construction.
- Mortar must be used within two hours and then left to set. It may be advantageous to brush the surface later the same day to expose the grit.
- Do not use if the temperature is too low i.e. 5°C or below.
- Be prepared to protect from frost, excessive sunlight and drying winds.
- Pointing must be kept moist for seven days at 10°C. Temperature variations will affect the speed of set. The chemical set can only complete in the presence of water.

It should be possible to build at about the same rate as normally expected rates for two storey buildings with Portland cement mortars but bear in mind the initial set is relatively slow and the mortar will continue to gain strength for many weeks.

9.3 Protection and aftercare for lime mortars

Effects of rain and temperature

Without doubt, often the most significant difference to the user between OPC (ordinary Portland cement) and lime-based mortars and renders is the rate of strength build up in cold weather. This can result in:

- Slower rate of laying;
- Requirement for protection against water saturation and frost.

This notwithstanding, in mild winter weather work with hydraulic lime mortars can proceed normally provided there is provision of immediately available protection in the event of rain and/or frost.

In order to understand the need for protection, specifiers and contractors should appreciate that the rate of set of hydraulic lime is more dependant on temperature than cement. While mortars laid in the summer months may achieve frost resistance in a month, work done in the cooler times of the year will undoubtedly take longer. As a result protection will be required for longer, perhaps for the remainder of the winter. The worst combination of ambient conditions is heavy rain followed by clear skies and a frost. Saturated walls with under-strength mortars will suffer frost damage much more easily than walls protected from the rain.

Driving rain poses less of a risk than rain entering from the top of the wall. As a result covers on the top of the wall overlapping, say 300 mm each side, will do much to keep the wall dry, thereby reducing the risk of damage.

Another factor to bear in mind relates to porosity of masonry units. Porous materials can hold very large quantities of water. Lime mortars are designed to aid evaporation. This process of evaporation causes a drop in temperature, so the mortar in new walls holding large quantities of water will set slower because of this drop in temperature. A great deal of the water in the masonry units will evaporate out through the mortar joints. This effect will ensure a permanently low temperature in the lime mortar until the whole wall begins to dry. Cement mortars are much less permeable and a high percentage of water will have to evaporate from the face of the masonry units.

Frost protection

As previously stated, wet masonry is much more vulnerable to frost. Frost protection of masonry is best achieved using hessian and bubble wrap or similar insulation. During daylight hours, if warming winter sun is available, covers should be lifted to allow heat to be absorbed and then replaced in the late afternoon. Even under these conditions it is important to maintain air circulation between the covers and the masonry.

9.4 Health and safety – natural hydraulic lime

Product
Natural hydraulic lime

General
Bags and delivery documents are labelled with a health and safety warning indicating that lime is an irritant.

Identification of substance
An odourless white powder. When mixed with sand and water it becomes a binder used for building applications.

Manufacturer
The name and address must be supplied on all bags.

Composition/information on ingredients
Chemical description: Principal constituent calcium hydroxide $Ca(OH)_2$ with calcium silicates, aluminates, ferro-aluminates and sulfates. Also small quantities of magnesium and other trace elements.
Hazardous ingredients: Calcium hydroxide, silicates and alkalis.

Hazard identification
Irritating to skin and eyes. Can cause burns in the presence of moisture. Product has a drying effect on the skin. When mixed with water a strong alkaline solution is produced which can cause chemical burns without pain being felt at the time.

First Aid measures
Eye contact: Wash eyes immediately with clean water for at least 20 minutes. **SEEK MEDICAL ATTENTION IMMEDIATELY.**
Skin contact: Wash affected area immediately with plenty of clean water. Remove contaminated clothing and wash before use.
Ingestion: Do not induce vomiting. Wash mouth with water and drink plenty of water. Seek medical advice if necessary.
Inhalation: Irrigate nose and throat with water for at least 20 minutes. It is advisable to seek medical attention. Remove patient from prolonged and repeated inhalation of high exposure.

Conservation

At Hardwick Hall, Derbyshire, records indicate that blue lias lime was used in the past. The garden walls are currently undergoing a phased programme of repairs and repointing with blue lias hydraulic lime. The mortar specified includes crushed and graded stone from the Hardwick Estate quarry to match the original aggregate. The new lime mortar incorporates the same aggregate throughout, but the specification has been varied to suit the different exposure conditions at copings, plane walling and adjacent to the ground.
Architects: Rodney Melville and Partners

Figure 1 *Hardwick Hall, detail of garden walls, prior to repair and repointing with blue lias hydraulic lime mortar (NHL 3.5).*

Figure 2 *(right) Hardwick Hall, detail of completed work on garden wall.*

Figure 3 *(below) Hardwick Hall, length of repaired and repointed garden wall.*

Richard's Castle, Shropshire retained sections of early lime render.
Architects: Rodney Melville and Partners

Figure 4 *Richard's Castle church tower, friable stone work before repair.*

Figure 5 *Richard's Castle church tower masonry repairs.*

Figure 6 *(above) Close-up of Richard's Castle showing tower wall render.*

Figure 7 *(left) Richard's Castle – Foresight members on site visit discussing conservation work to masonry pointing and render.*

Figure 8 *Private house, Dorset, raking out joints prior to repointing with 1:3 hydraulic lime mix.*

Figure 9 *1:3 hydraulic lime mix for repointing mill building in figure 8 using well-graded sharp sand containing 4 mm grit.*

New build work

Hydraulic limes have been successfully used on many recent new builds, providing long-term advantages in terms of water vapour permeability and acceptance of thermal movement.

Figure 10 *(above) New science block, Sherborne Boys School. Blue lias hydraulic lime used throughout.*

Figure 11 *(left) Early stages of construction of new science block, Sherborne Boys School. Note consistency of mortar on the board.*

Figure 12 *Construction of RSPB Headquarters building at Sandy, Bedfordshire using a hydraulic lime mortar with 'coarse stuff', 1996.*

Figure 13 *Detail of brickwork at RSPB Headquarters showing joints slightly raked back.*

Figure 14 *New Government offices, Sheperds Wharf, Plymouth. Hydraulic lime mortar plus local limestone reclaimed from original dock buildings. Built 1996.*

Figure 15 *(left) New cottages in traditional design, Dorset, built with hydraulic lime throughout.*

Figure 16 *(below) Palladian style mansion in Wiltshire, built with hydraulic lime throughout, completed 2002.*

Figure 17 *Hydraulic lime mortars for load-bearing walls using insulating block and internal concrete block walls.*

Figure 18 *Foresight team on a site visit to examine mortars.*

Figures 19a and 19b
Mortars using the same ingredients but different water quantities, figure 19a (above left) prepared by stone masons, figure 19b (above right) prepared by bricklayers.

Figure 20 *(left) A warning! New brickwork suffering severe frost damage due to bad site practice.*

Fire fighting measures

Natural hydraulic lime is not combustible

Accidental release measures

Personal precautions: See exposure controls and personal protection. *Cleaning up:* Contain spillage and keep the material dry if possible. Minimize air borne dust and avoid contamination of drains or watercourses. In the event of spillage into watercourses the Environmental Agency must be alerted. Keep children away during clean-up operation.

Storage and handling

Storage: Bags should be stacked in a safe and stable manner. Keep separate from flammable materials and chemicals with which it might react.
Handling: Appropriate manual handling techniques should be adhered to in accordance with the relevant Manual Handling Operations' Regulations. Personal protective equipment should be worn to satisfy the advice given in the *exposure controls and personal protection* section of this report.
General: Bags should be handled with care to avoid damage to bags and the generation of dust.

Exposure control/personal protection

Occupational exposure limit (OEL): Recommended limit 4 mg/m^3 (8hr/TWA)
Respiratory protection: If atmospheric dust levels exceed the OEL, approved dust respirators should be used to ensure that exposure is below the OEL.
Eye protection: Dust proof anti-fog goggles should be used to prevent dust and lime/water mixture entering the eyes.
Skin: Protective clothing should be worn to prevent both dust and lime/water mixture contacting the skin. Long-sleeved overalls/waterproofs, boots and rubber or fabric/composite gloves should be worn as appropriate.

Physical/chemical properties

Physical data:

Physical state	particulate – fine dry powder
Odour	possible earthy odour
Colour	cream
pH	12 (approx) as aqueous solution
Bulk density	600 kg/m^3
Solubility in water	1.76 g/l saturated solution at 10°C

Chemical composition:

Mainly a mixture of	CaO, SiO_2, Al_2O_3, Fe_2O_3, MgO, K_2O, SO_3

Stability and reactivity

Stable. Avoid exposure to moisture. Reacts to acids with the evolution of heat.

Toxicological information

Short term effect of over exposure:

Eye contact	Can be very painful. May cause partial or total loss of sight if untreated.
Skin contact	Irritating to skin. May cause burns in the presence of moisture.
Ingestion	Causes corrosion of, and damage to gastrointestinal tract.
Inhalation	Irritant to respiratory tract.

Long term effects: May cause irritation to skin and dermatitis. Prolonged and repeated inhalation of high concentration may damage the respiratory tract.

Ecological information

Mobility: Soluble in water as calcium hydroxide to form alkaline solution

Persistence and degradability: Non-biodegradable – reacts with atmospheric carbon dioxide to form calcium carbonate (limestone)

Bio accumulative potential: Aquatic toxicity – non-toxic LC50 aquatic toxicity values are >100Mg/l. PH – 12 (approx) as aqueous solution. Solubility in water 1.76 g/l saturated solution at 10°C.

Disposal conditions

Natural hydraulic lime and packaging should be disposed of only at appropriately licensed waste facilities. Disposal should be in accordance with local and national legislation.

Transport information

Classification of conveyance – none. Not classified as hazardous for transport by road or rail.

Regulatory Information

The Chemicals (Hazard Information and Packaging) Regulations 1993 Statutory Instrument 1746.

Classification for supply – Irritant

Risk phases	Irritating to skin (R38)
	Risk of serious damage to eyes(R41)
Safety phases	Do not breathe dust (S22)
	Wear eye/face protection (S39)
	In case of contact with eyes, rinse immediately with plenty of water and seek medical advice (S26)

Legislation and other information

- Health and Safety at Work Act 1974
- Control of Substances Hazardous to Health (Regulations) 1988
- HSE Occupational Exposure Criteria Document Summaries 1993 Edition
- HSE Guidance Note EH26 (Occupational Skin Diseases – Health and Safety Precautions) (HMSO 1981)
- HSE Guidance Note EH 40 (Occupational Exposure Limits)
- Any authorized manual on First Aid by St John's Ambulance, St Andrew's and the Red Cross
- Manual Handling Operations Regulations 1992
- Environmental Protection Act

Product name: Mixed sharp sand to BS1200:1976 Type 'S'		
Petrological name: Flint/quartz		
Mechanical analysis:		
B.S. sieve (mm + 0.001 mm)	% passing	BS 1200 'S'
10 mm	100	100
5 mm	100	98–100
2.36 mm	90	90–100
1.18 mm	76	70–100
600 mm	51	40–100
300 mm	26	5–70
150 mm	8	0–15
75 mm	1.5	0–5
Chemical analysis:		
Silica	SiO_2	97.39%
Alumina	Al_2O_3	0.20%
Iron oxide	Fe_2O_3	0.81%
Titania	TiO_2	0.05%
Calcium oxide	CaO	0.26%
Magnesium oxide	MgO	0.30%
Potassium oxide	K_2O	0.14%
Sodium oxide	Na_2O	0.02%
Manganese	MnO	0.05%
Loss on ignition		0.67%
Physical properties:		
Relative density (oven dried)		2.54
Relative density (saturated surface dry)		2.57
Relative density (apparent)		2.60
Water absorption		0.99%

Figure 8 *Technical data sheet mixed sharp sand – typical values.*

Bibliography

BS EN 459: Part 1: 2001. Building lime – definitions, specifications and conformity criteria.

BS EN 459: Part 2: 2001. Building lime – test methods.

BS 812. Testing aggregates. Part 103: 1985. Method for determination of particle size distribution.

BS EN 998: Part 2: 2002. Specification for mortar for masonry.

BS EN 1008: 2002. Mixing water for concrete.

BS 1199 / BS 1200: 1976. (Superseded by BS EN 13139.) Specifications for building sands from natural sources.

BS 1200: 1996. Sands for mortar for plain and reinforced brickwork, blockwalling and masonry.

BS 3148: 1980. Water for making concrete (including notes on the suitability of the water).

BS 3921: 1995. Specification for clay bricks.

BS 4551. Part 1: 1998. Methods of testing mortars – physical testing.

BS 5628. Part 1: 1992. Code of practice for use of masonry – structural use of unreinforced masonry.

BS 5628. Part 3: 2001. Code of practice for use of masonry – materials and components, design and workmanship.

BS 8104: 1992. Code of practice for assessing exposure of walls to wind-driven rain.

BS EN ISO 9002: 1994. Quality systems. Model for quality assurance in design, development, production, installation and servicing.

BS EN 13139: 2002. Aggregates for mortar.

Building Research Establishment Digest 127. An index of exposure to driving rain.

Further Reading

Chapman, S. and Fidler, J. (eds.), *English Heritage Directory of Building Sands and Aggregates*, Donhead Publishing, Shaftesbury, 2000.

Cowper, A.D., *Lime and Lime Mortar*, facsimile of 1927 edition, Donhead Publishing, Shaftesbury, 1997.

Dimes, F.G. and Ashurst, J., *Conservation of Building and Decorative Stone*, Butterworth-Heinemann, Oxford, 1998.

Gibbons, P., *Preparation and Use of Lime Mortars*, Historic Scotland, Edinburgh, revised 1995.

Hill, P.R. and David, J.C.E., *Practical Stone Masonry*, Donhead Publishing, London, 1995.

Historic Scotland, *Traditional Building Materials*, Conference Proceedings, Historic Scotland, 1997.

Holmes, S. and Wingate, M., *Building with Lime*, Intermediate Technology Publications, 1995, revised 2002.

Howe, J.A., *The Geology of Building Stones*, facsimile of 1910 edition, Donhead Publishing, Shaftesbury, 2001.

Leslie, A., and Gibbons, P., *Scottish Aggregates for Building Conservation*, Historic Scotland, 1999.

Lynch, G., *Brickwork*, Volumes 1 and 2, Donhead Publishing, Shaftesbury, 1994.

Lynch, G., *Gauged Brickwork*, Donhead Publishing, Shaftesbury, first published by Gower, Aldershot, 1990.

Nash, W.G., *Brickwork Repair and Restoration*, second edition, Attic Books, Las Vegas, 1989.

Pasley, C., *Observations on Lime*, facsimile of 1838 edition, Donhead Publishing, Shaftesbury, 1997.

Pepperell, R., *Stonemasonry Detailing*, Attic Books, Las Vegas, 1990.

Schofield, J., *Lime in Building*, Black Dog Press, Crendon, 1995.

Teutonico, J.M. (ed.), *English Heritage Directory of Building Limes*, Donhead Publishing, Shaftesbury, 1997.

Warren, J., *Conservation of Brick*, Butterworth-Heinemann, Oxford, 1999.

Vicat, L.J. (Trans. Smith, Capt. J.T.), *Mortars and Cements*, facsimile of 1837 edition, Donhead Publishing, Shaftesbury 1997.

Glossary

Addition: finely divided inorganic material used in order to improve or achieve special properties. It can be active, e.g. possess pozzolanic properties or inert, e.g. filler or pigment.

Aggregate: the hard filler materials, such as sand and stone, in mortars, plasters, renders and concretes.

Air lime: lime that sets through carbonation rather than reaction with water.

Air-entraining agent: materials that cause air to be included in a mortar mix. The size and spacing of the air bubbles will determine their influence on mortar properties.

Alite: tri-calcium silicate, the main reactive constituent of Portland cement, formed by heating siliceous limestone to high (above 1200°C) temperatures. Not present in significant amounts in natural hydraulic limes of low hydraulicity but found in increasing amounts as hydraulicity increases.

Aluminates: compounds of aluminium and oxygen, usually with lime or silica.

Argillaceous: containing clay minerals, normally used in the context of rocks or marls.

Ashlar: squared and regular masonry.

Batch, batching: the constituents making up a single load for mixer, the process of adding the constituent materials to the mixer in the prescribed quantities.

Belite: di-calcium silicate, the main reactive constituent in hydraulic limes, also present as a component of Portland cement where it reacts much more slowly than does alite.

Binder: the material which forms the matrix between aggregate particles in a mortar, plaster, render or concrete. It is a fluid paste when first prepared, but must then harden to hold the aggregate in a coherent state. Usually applied to calcium lime, hydraulic lime, cement and gypsum and to combinations of these with pozzolans.

Bleeding: a process in fresh mortar whereby water separates from the mix due to lack of cohesion and faulty mix design.

Block: a masonry unit.

Bond: in this context the adhesion between two surfaces, for example the mortar and the masonry unit.

Brick: fired clay masonry units.

Brittle: the tendency to crack when subjected to flexural loading.

Bulking: the property of sands to increase in volume when wetted hence reducing bulk density leading to batching errors when batching by volume without compensation.

Burning: the thermal process of heating material, usually in a kiln, to expel water and cause a change in mineralogy, e.g. converting argillaceous limestone to hydraulic lime.

Calcite: the mineral form of calcium carbonate having a rhombohedral crystal structure. It is the common form found in carbonated lime mortar to which it gives strength. It occurs naturally as Iceland Spar and has a unique double refraction of light which is suggested to be the reason for the exceptional appearance of limewashed surfaces.

Calcium: a soft white metallic element, more normally occurring as the oxide, hydroxide, carbonate or other compound.

Calcium aluminates: minerals formed when aluminous clays are burnt with limestone, the major ones being tri-calcium aluminate, tetra-calcium alumino ferrite or 'brownmillerite' and di-calcium alumino silicate or 'gehlenite'.

Calcium carbonate: a material composed of calcium oxide combined with carbon dioxide from which lime is prepared. Natural forms are limestones, chalks, shells and corals. It is also formed as an industrial by-product, as in the manufacture of acetylene. Mortars, renders, plasters and concretes containing calcium hydroxide take up carbon dioxide from the air to form calcium carbonate, the method by which air limes develop strength.

Calcium hydroxide: a material composed of calcium oxide combined with water and the chemical name for slaked or hydrated lime, lime putty and milk of lime, depending on the residual moisture content.

Calcium lime: the new term introduced by BS EN 459-1 referring to quicklime, calcium hydroxide as a dry powder (*see* hydrated lime) or putty. Often referred to as air lime.

Calcium oxide: referred to as quicklime, having a chemical composition of one part calcium to one part oxygen.

Calcium silicates: minerals formed when clays or other siliceous materials are burnt with limestone. Belite, di-calcium silicate, is the slower reacting of these and converts to the more reactive alite, tri-calcium silicate, when burnt with available lime at higher temperatures. They react with water, hydraulic reaction, to form the main cementing compounds of hydraulic lime and cement mortars and concretes.

Carbonation, carbonated: the process of forming carbonates, in this context the formation of calcium carbonate from calcium hydroxide. An air lime mortar is said to have carbonated when the binder has reacted with carbon dioxide from the air to form calcium carbonate and developed strength beyond that which is achieved simply by drying out.

Carbonic acid: the very weak acid which is formed when carbon dioxide gas dissolves in water. The salts of this acid are the carbonates and the bicarbonates.

Cement: a quick-setting binder for making mortars, renders, plasters and concretes. The most widespread cement is Portland cement. Also applied to so-called Roman and other natural cements, more correctly termed hydraulic limes, historically prepared by burning calcareous clays or nodules of calcareous clay (such as Septaria or rock formations of similar composition). The distinction between these and other hydraulic limes is that the cements must be ground to a fine powder before they can react quickly with water.

Chalk: a common form of calcium carbonate with a very fine structure. A limestone of cretaceous age, usually very porous and ranging from white to pale grey in colour.

Class A limes: are non-hydraulic, air limes otherwise known as rich or fat limes. High purity in terms of calcium oxide content and generally white in colour, but colour is not a good guide to quality. Now re-classified as calcium limes (CL90) in BS EN 459-1.

Class B limes: are non-hydraulic limes produced from less pure limestones or chalks. They are burnt at low temperatures which are insufficient to convert the argillaceous components to hydraulic compounds but might activate them to give pozzolanic activity, which gives a slight and slow hydraulic set. Now re-classified as calcium limes (CL70 or CL80) in BS EN 459-1.

Class C limes: are naturally occurring hydraulic limes containing an appreciable amount of active clay which can confer hydraulic properties so that it sets when in the presence of water. Now re-classified as natural hydraulic lime (NHL) in BS EN 459-1 with values, 2, 3.5 or 5, depending on their hydraulic reactivity.

Clay: the fine particles produced by the weathering of rocks, each particle being less than two microns in diameter. They are chemically alumino-silicates and physically take the form of thin plates, which stack together.

Clinker, cement clinker: a hard solid material formed by the fusion of liquid phases and crystalline cement compounds when cement materials are burnt at high temperature.

Compressive strength: the property of a hardened mortar or concrete to resist compressive forces and can be expressed as pounds per square inch, newtons per millimetre square or mega-pascals per millimetre square. (the last two are numerically identical i.e. the conversion is one).

Consistence: a measure of workability of a mortar such that it is capable of being transported, placed and finished easily and without segregation.

Construction: the overall structure consisting of several elements, each of which should be considered separately as to the exposure, durability and physical requirements to be taken into account when specifying materials.

Cure: the setting and hardening process of a plastic mix containing a cementitious binder.

Durability: the ability of a construction to resist the degradation by environmental conditions and decay mechanisms during its design life.

Eminently hydraulic lime: previously class C3 lime, now re-classified by BS EN 459-1 as NHL 3.5 and NHL 5 which overlap. The traditional

C3 eminently hydraulic lime maximum anticipated compressive strength was 10 N/mm^2. The maximum for NHL 5 is an average of 15 N/mm^2 with a maximum of 20 N/mm^2 at 28 days. It is prepared from a limestone containing a high proportion of active clay. Most suitable for hydraulic engineering works. The distinction between this and a natural cement is that an eminently hydraulic lime still contains enough free lime to enable it to break up and slake when water is added, whereas the cement requires fine grinding to enable it to hydrate.

Fair-faced: the exposed face of an element which has received special finishing, or surface coating or care in the use of natural materials, to enhance its appearance.

Fat lime: previously class A lime putty having good workability, now re-classified by BS EN 459-1 as calcium lime (CL90).

Feebly hydraulic lime: slightly hydraulic lime, previously the traditional class C1 lime. It contains a small amount of active clay, typically less than 12 per cent, and should set in water in fifteen to twenty days, or even longer. The anticipated compressive strength of C1 was 1.3 to 2 N/mm^2. This is below the strength requirement for the new BS EN 459 classification for NHL, which is from 2 to 7 N/mm^2. It therefore appears that there is no current standard to adequately cover the traditional feebly (slightly) hydraulic lime class C1.

Filler: ground limestone or other inert mineral, having at least the fineness of cement, and used to supplement the void filling ability of lean mixes.

Flexural strength: the property of a hardened mortar or concrete to resist flexural forces and can be expressed as pounds per square inch, newtons per millimetre square or mega-pascals per millimetre square. (The last two are numerically identical i.e. the conversion is one).

Flocculation: the gathering together or clotting of fine particles from a dispersed state to form large agglomerations.

Fly ash: a very fine ash collected by the exhaust filters of boilers or furnaces, usually in the power generation industry. Such ashes have glass phases with pozzolanic properties depending on the composition and burning temperature.

Free lime: lime in a mortar or hydraulic lime which remains as calcium hydroxide and has not yet carbonated or combined with a pozzolan or other minerals or compounds. It is more soluble than calcium carbonate and can be transported within the pore solution and is available for deposition to heal fine cracks – autogenous healing. Not to be confused with free lime present as calcium oxide in Portland cement, which is of much lower quantity and is a measure of the efficiency of burning, i.e. low free lime equals well-burnt Portland cement.

Frog: an indentation in the bearing surface of a brick to improve the bond with mortar and increase resistance to lateral forces. The indentation can be in one or both bearing surfaces. If only in one, the best resistance to lateral force is achieved when the brick is placed with its frog uppermost.

Frost resistance: the ability to resist a given number of freezing and thawing cycles, depending on the anticipated exposure environment.

Galleting: insertion of small pieces of stone or tile into mortar on the face of walls to bring forward eroded surfaces to assist in making good and/or pin between larger units.

Gauge: a container of specified volume by which the quantity of a mortar constituent can be measured during batching.

Grading: the proportion by mass of an aggregate in various size fractions.

Granulated blastfurnace slag: a glassy, calcium alumino silicate material formed by rapidly quenching the slag from an iron-making blastfurnace. When ground to cement fineness it will have pozzolanic properties dependent on its chemistry and the effectiveness of the quenching.

Grit: fine aggregate produced by crushing and/or sieving natural rock or fine gravel.

Harden: the process by which mortar or plaster loses its plasticity, either by loss of water to the masonry or air, by the onset of hydraulic set, by carbonation, or a combination of them.

HLM: abbreviation for hydraulic lime mortar.

Hydrated lime, (1) dry hydrate: calcium hydroxide as a dry powder. The heat generated by the slaking process is used to drive off any excess moisture before it is packed in containers, usually paper sacks, or distributed in bulk tankers. (2) **lime putty:** calcium hydroxide as a putty.

Hydraulic binder: a binder which sets and develops strength by chemical reaction with water such that it can set under water.

Hydraulic lime: natural hydraulic limes class, NHL, prepared by burning limestones or chalks that contain clayey impurities. They consist mainly of calcium silicates and aluminates together with an excess of free lime. Having the property of setting and hardening under water. Carbonation by reaction with atmospheric carbon dioxide also contributes to the hardening process. Artificial hydraulic limes, class HLZ, may contain added hydraulic or pozzolanic material, including Portland cement. Hydraulic limes are most useful in conditions subject to frequent saturation or continuous damp, and for hydraulic engineering works such as canals, harbour walls or bridge piers.

Hydraulic lime mortar: The mixture of an hydraulic lime with aggregate and water.

Joint: the space between masonry units, usually filled with mortar to evenly spread the vertical loads, improve resistance to lateral loads and control moisture ingress.

Kiln: a structure of brick or stone, or metal lined with brick, in which material is heated to effect chemical reaction, such as calcinations of lime by driving off carbon dioxide in calcium carbonate.

Knocking-up: the process of re-working a mortar that has been previously mixed and left to stand before use. For mortars containing hydraulic lime this should only be permitted when the workability can be restored without adding significant amounts of water.

Lime putty: slaked lime, which has been stored in excess of water to fatten up. This process also enables less reactive particles to be hydrated before use. In Roman times the lime putty for plastering of the highest standard had to be stored for three years before use. A distinction is often drawn between putty prepared from dry hydrate and putty run from quicklime. The latter is considered superior where plasticity and good carbonation is needed. The difference is due to the different crystal size and shape. Well-matured putty disagglomerates, dissolves and re-precipitates during storage to give a finer product. Dry hydrate is composed mostly of much coarser particles and needs to be made into putty and matured before use to give best results.

Limestone: any rock or stone whose main constituents are calcium and/or magnesium carbonates.

Masonry: assemblage of units of brick, stone or block set in mortar.

Masonry units: brick, stone or block from which a wall is constructed.

Maturity: the degree to which mortar has progressed towards full hydration. The rate is affected by temperature, increasing as temperature increases and slowed if humidity falls. Also affected by the presence of accelerators or retarders.

Metakaolin: a highly reactive alumino silicate pozzolan produced by calcining china clay.

Microsilica, silica fume: a highly reactive ultra-fine siliceous pozzolan, a by-product of the ferrosilicon industry.

Moderately hydraulic lime: the traditional class C2 lime with anticipated compressive strength of 2 to 6 N/mm^2. The class NHL 3.5 natural hydraulic lime covers this but gives a much wider range for compressive strength between 3.5 to 10 N/mm^2 with an upper limit of 14 N/mm^2 at 28 days. Class C2 lime is expected to set under water in about six to eight days, but possibly longer.

Mortar: a building material, usually consisting of sand, a binder and water, in a plastic state which can be trowelled, becomes hard in place, and which can be used for bedding and jointing masonry units.

NHL: abbreviation for natural hydraulic lime.

Natural hydraulic lime: hydraulic lime produced by burning a mixture of naturally occurring argillaceous limestone, or chalk. In BS EN 459-1 they are given the designation of NHL together with a numerical value (2, 3.5 or 5) depending on their hydraulic reactivity.

Non-hydraulic lime: a high purity, generally calcareous lime, CL90, but can be dolomitic.

OPC: abbreviation for ordinary Portland cement, *see* Portland cement.

PFA: abbreviation for pulverized-fuel ash, *see* fly ash.

Particle size distribution: the proportions of different sized fractions in a material. In the case of a sand used for mortar, best results are obtained with sands having an even distribution between at least four fraction sizes.

Permeability: the ease with which a liquid or vapour can pass through a solid material.

Phenolphthalein indicator: a widely available chemical indicator which can clearly differentiate between acid and alkaline conditions. Thus on calcium carbonate it remains colourless whilst on calcium hydroxide it changes to deep purple-red. When sprayed onto a freshly fractured mortar section it can show the extent of carbonation.

Pigment: colouring material from which decorative paints, mortars, renders and concretes can be made. They can be dry powder or dispersed in water and, for use in lime mortars, should be stable in alkaline conditions.

Pinnings: small stones placed in joints to stabilize masonry and reduce the volume of mortar required.

Plastic state: the initial wet state of a mortar whilst still workable.

Porosity: the extent to which a solid material has pores or voids.

Portland cement: made by sintering a precisely specified mixture of raw materials (raw meal, paste or slurry) containing elements, usually expressed as oxides, CaO, SiO_2, Al_2O_3, Fe_2O_3 and small quantities of other materials. This hydraulic clinker consists of at least two-thirds by mass of calcium silicates ($3CaO \cdot SiO_2$ and $2CaO \cdot SiO_2$), the remainder consisting of aluminium and iron containing clinker phases and other compounds. The clinker is finely ground, with a few percent of gypsum to control early setting, intimately mixed and despatched in bulk or packed into paper sacks. Now designated CEM I in accordance with BS EN 197-1.

Pozzolan, pozzolanic material: a material containing constituents, generally reactive aluminates and silicates, which will combine with lime at normal temperatures in the presence of moisture to form stable binding hydrates. It may be used with a fat lime to give hydraulic properties to a mortar. Fine grinding improves their reactivity but can also, with porous materials, increase the water demand thereby negating some, or even all, of the strength gain.

Pozzolana: a pozzolanic material of volcanic origin from the Pozzuoli district near Mount Vesuvius, Italy. It was used in classical mortars and has given its name to the generic pozzolans.

Protection: covering over the finished work to resist the effect of ambient conditions freezing or drying out the mortar until the hydraulic reaction and/or carbonation is sufficiently mature to be self-protecting.

Putty: *see* lime putty.

Quicklime: lime which has been burnt but not slaked. Called 'quick' because of its lively affinity for water. Can be produced in various combinations of calcium oxide, magnesium oxide or a mixed calcium-magnesium oxide and in a range of sizes from powder, through pebble to large lump.

Reactivity (of lime): the ability of a lime to react quickly in chemical reactions, particularly with water in the slaking process. It is partly dependent on the parent limestone and largely depends on the temperature and duration of calcination. Reactive limes have porous structures with high surface areas, hard-burnt limes are less reactive and over-burnt or dead-burnt limes are very unreactive.

Render: a specially formulated plastering mortar applied externally.

Re-working: the process of re-working a mortar, which has been previously mixed and left to stand before use. For mortars containing hydraulic lime this should be permitted only when the workability can be restored without adding significant amounts of water.

Rich mortar: one with a higher than normal proportion of binder to aggregate or with a particularly smooth binder. It would be particularly free-flowing and easy to use but, unless water content is carefully controlled, can be more prone to shrinkage.

Rubble walling: walling built of rough-faced stones not dressed to give fine joints but sometimes squared and coursed. *See also* ashlar.

Sand: weathered or crushed particles of rocks, usually high in silica, smaller than gravels and larger than silts, typically between 0.06 mm and 5 mm. The particles should be hard and not crumble under abrasion. Sand is used as the aggregate in mortars, renders and plasters and as a component of concrete.

Salt: a chemical compound formed when an acid reacts with an alkali. Salts are named according to the acid and the alkali metal from which they are formed so that calcium sulfate was formed, either in nature or an industrial process, by the action of sulfuric acid or one of its derivatives on a calcium compound.

Set: the state at which the paste will resist the force of a standard probe. When applied to hydraulic lime it is the time when the matrix of hydrates becomes continuous. When applied to mortar it can also include the stiffening effect through loss of moisture.

Shrinkage: contraction in size, usually through drying, and a main cause of cracking in mortar, render and plaster, which is not protected until it has sufficient strength to resist the contraction forces.

Silicates: the most common form of silica occurring in natural rocks making up 95 per cent of the earth's crust. Also formed when siliceous materials are thermally treated in the presence of calcium, magnesium and aluminium compounds as in hydraulic lime production.

Siliceous: material containing silicon, usually as its oxide, silica, or some compound of that.

Silt: clay and fine particles below 75 microns in aggregate which reduces strength and durability by increasing the water demand and preventing good bonding between binder and aggregate surfaces. A simple field settling test is available for routine site control.

Sintered: brought to a sufficiently high temperature for the material to begin to fuse into a single mass.

Slaked lime: calcium hydroxide formed by the action of water on quicklime.

Slaking: the action of quicklime reacting with water. In the presence of an excess of water a putty is formed and where water is controlled to the minimum, dry hydrate is formed. Slaking will also take place when quicklime is exposed to air, but the effectiveness is controlled by air volume and moisture content.

Stiffening: the early stage of a mortar when workability has been lost, mainly through water reduction by suction into the masonry units.

Stone: masonry unit of natural rock.

Suction: the drawing-in of pore water from mortar into masonry, which improves the bond but, if not controlled, results in rapid loss of mortar workability and ultimate strength or even failure of the mortar.

Sulfate-resistance: the ability of a binder or mortar to resist expansion due to reaction with natural sulfate salts.

Tile: fired clay products for roofing, floors and walls.

Tile slips: small pieces of tile for insertion into mortar on the face of walls to bring forward eroded surfaces to assist in making good.

Trass: a pozzolanic material of volcanic origin from the Rhine valley.

Voids: the space left between sand grains and/or aggregate particles which has to be filled with a paste of binder and water to achieve a mortar that is workable and durable.

Water retention: the ability of a mortar to retain its water against the suction forces from the masonry units. To an extent the absorption of water from mortar improves the bond between masonry and mortar. However, if water is lost too quickly the mortar becomes unworkable and the quality of the masonry deteriorates.

Workability: the ease with which a mortar may be used. This important property is not easily defined, but it includes high plasticity and good water retention. A highly plastic binder, such as good lime putty or high calcium hydraulic lime, can allow the use of much sharper sands than are possible with, say, a cement binder. These sharp sands contribute to the long-term durability.

Appendix A
Scheme for Assessment of Conformity of Site-made Mortar

A.1 General

It is rarely economic to install all of the sampling and testing procedures on site to ensure that all of the required properties of the mortars are being achieved (e.g. durability, permeability, plasticity). In most cases it will be sufficient to check that good practice is being applied on site and that the mix proportions are being batched using approved gauges. Where more detailed monitoring is justified, the strength of mortar produced on site provides a relatively simple means of ensuring that the mortar is consistent with the specified mortar. The following scheme will ensure that significant departures from the specified mortar are detected and provide sufficient information and/or samples for the degree of failure and its consequences to be determined.

A.2 Trial mixes and base data

The essential characteristics of the specified mortar should be established to the extent necessary to subsequently monitor conformity. Such procedures might include:

- Where batching is by volume, use the same gauge during tests as that to be used on site and determine the weight of the contents.
- Record the mass of each constituent
- Measure the moisture content of the sand and the effect of moisture variation on the mass of sand from the gauge determined.

- Prepare the mortar using the mixer type, addition sequence and mixing time specified for the site.
- Agree the mortar workability with the contractor and record this together with the method of measurement e.g. flow table, dropping ball etc.
- Use BS 4551 Clause 10 for determining the plastic density and air content.
- Demoulding times may be increased to seven days to prevent damage to weaker mortars.
- Test for density and compressive strength at 28 and 91 days. Sample mortars, prepare test specimens in steel moulds and cure in accordance with BS 4551.

A.3 Assessment of site mortars

When assessing site mortar for conformity with the specification, sample mortar and prepare test specimens as detailed in A.2. In addition carry out as much of the following as is relevant to the specification:

- Check workability of mortar being used on site.
- Monitor site storage temperatures of test specimens.
- Forward samples for laboratory test as soon as they are sufficiently set to prevent distortion of their shape.
- From a different mortar batch keep each material separate, pack into labelled plastic bags before forwarding to the laboratory. This is for comparison with samples prepared in accordance with A2 above.
- Demoulding, curing and testing to be in accordance with A2 above.

Any variation in compressive strength greater than 35% of the A2 28 day value or 20% at 91 days would normally be considered significant and warrant investigation. Causes of variations could be:

- Significant variation in sand moisture or grading.
- Variations in batch weight.
- Significant changes in plastic density and /or air content.
- Changes in constituent materials.
- Temperature variations during site or laboratory storage.
- Errors in test procedure.

The information contained in the above scheme should be adequate to establish causes of variations and for its significance on the performance in service to be established.

Appendix B
Additions

B.1 Pozzolans

Hydraulic reactivity

The reactivity of pozzolans can be determined in a number of ways, mostly based on their combination with calcium hydroxide. The practical implications of reactivity can be determined by testing the strength of mortar containing the pozzolan and made up to the standard workability used for a hydraulic lime mortar. The reactivity can be gauged against the amount of additional hydraulic lime to achieve an equivalent strength. This method takes into account any change in water demand of the mix arising from the use of the pozzolan. It also allows an assessment of the performance of the mix in terms of durability compared with hydraulic lime mixes. In assessing the performance of pozzolan-modified mixes attention has to be given to any change in the density of the mortar and any constituent of the pozzolan that might affect resistance to chemical agents.

Table B1 sets out the reactivity of various pozzolans tested in 1:3 mixes with NHL 3.5 natural hydraulic lime during the Foresight project. In some cases the hydraulic reactivity is negative, this usually relates to an increase in water demand of the mix in conjunction with only limited reactivity.

Some pozzolans, such as microsilica, granulated slag and metakaolin reduce in reactivity with time, possibly by exhausting available lime. Others, such as brick dust, fly ash and trass/pozzolana increase in

Pozzolan type	Addition rate (% v:v of NHL)	Reactivity (Factor for equivalent weight of NHL 3.5)			
		@ 28 days	@ 56 days	@ 91 days	@ 182 days
Metakaolin	10 20 30	10 10 13	10 10 10	7 8 9	8 8 9
Yellow brick dust (fine)	10 20 30	-1 0 0	0 1 1	0 0 1	0 1 1
Red brick dust (fine)	10 20 30	-1 0 0	0 0 0	0 0 0	0 1 1
Red brick dust (medium)	10 20 30	-1 0 0	0 0 0	0 0 0	0 1 1
Red brick dust (coarse)	10 20 30	-1 0 0	0 0 0	0 0 0	0 0 0
Granulated blastfurnace slag	10 20 30	7 8 7	6 6 6	4 5 4	4 4 4
Fly ash	10 20 30	-1 0 0	1 1 2	1 1 2	2 3 3
Dutch trass	10 20 30	-1 0 1	0 1 1	0 1 1	0 1 1
Italian pozzolana (coarse)	10 20 30	-1 -1 0	-1 0 1	0 1 1	0 1 2
Italian Pozzolana (ground)	10 20 30	0 0 0	0 1 2	0 1 2	0 1 2
Microsilica	10 20 30	8 10 10	8 8 8	6 7 6	7 7 6

Table B1 *Compressive strength reactivity of pozzolans in the Foresight project.*

reactivity with time. Pozzolans with high water absorption, such as trass and pozzolana, appear to increase in reactivity with increasing proportions of pozzolan.

Hardened properties

Pozzolans modify the microstructure of the mortar. Those having strong hydraulicity increase and densify the paste structure reducing permeability and increasing brittleness. Mortars containing more than 20 per cent of metakaolin or microsilica by volume of lime can become less permeable and more brittle than Portland cement mortars.

The chemical composition of some pozzolans can affect mortar durability. Metakaolin, with its high proportion of reactive alumina, can significantly reduce the sulfate resistance of lime mortars. Other pozzolans affected the durability of mortars in proportion to their hydraulic effect on strength. Porous pozzolans, added to mortars to increase permeability, slightly reduce strength.

B.2 Calcium lime

The use of calcium lime as replacement for, or to amend the properties of, hydraulic lime has been examined. Figure B1 shows the effect of the replacement level (% by mass) on compressive strength of a mortar with binder content equal to the mass of hydraulic lime plus calcium lime. There is an initial reduction in strength since the CL90 calcium lime used had a greater water demand compared with NHL 3.5. The figure should allow the effect of calcium lime, so-called 'gauging', on compressive strength to be estimated. The effect on flexural strength was not so marked so that plasticity, as estimated by the ratio of flexural strength to compressive strength was increased by approximately 20 per cent compared with the same compressive strength from the hydraulic lime alone. Plastic properties were generally improved by the addition of calcium lime resulting in a 'creamier' consistence.

Freeze/thaw resistance of mortars with added calcium lime was similar to hydraulic lime mortars of equivalent compressive strength. Resistance to sulfates was good. Carbonation and capillary permeability were marginally improved.

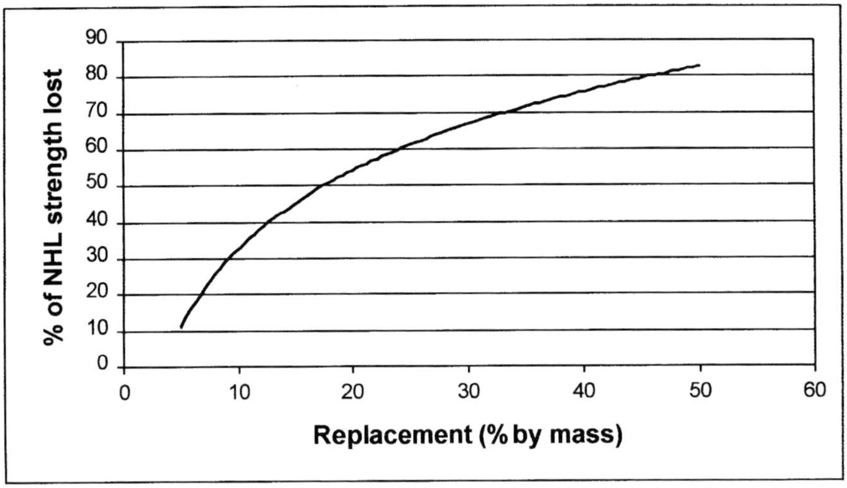

Figure B1 *Effect on compressive strength of replacement of NHL 3.5 with calcium lime.*

On the basis of these tests there are some advantages to be obtained from the addition of calcium lime to mortars where reduction in strength and resistance to freeze/thaw is taken into account in the mortar design.

B.3 Lime putty

The performance of hydraulic lime mortars with an addition of lime putty was in line with the observations for addition of calcium lime. The added water effect was generally greater, reflecting the increased water demand. Properties of plastic mortar showed an increase in the 'creaminess' and consistence, even over mortars having calcium lime addition.

B.4 Filler

The performance of hydraulic lime mortars containing fine filler, generally chalk or ground limestone, was similar to mortars with increased sand fine fraction. Plastic properties were improved, compared with mortars where the sand was deficient in fines, but water demand was increased and strengths reduced compared with mortars with well-graded sand. For design purposes it is recommended that filler be treated as part of the aggregate.

Appendix C
Microstructure of Mortars

Figure C1 *Mortar structure for 1:3 NHL 3.5.*

Scanning electron micrographs courtesy of the Interface Analysis Centre, Bristol University.

Figure C2 *Mortar structure for 1:6 NHL 3.5 lime showing more open texture.*

Figure C3 *Mortar structure for 1:1½ NHL 3.5 lime showing more dense structure.*

Figure C4 *Mortar structure for 1:3 NHL 3.5 lime with 30 per cent metakaolin showing more dense and complex structure.*

Figure C5 *Mortar structure for 1:3 NHL 3.5 lime with 5% lime putty showing more open structure with calcium hydroxide crystals.*

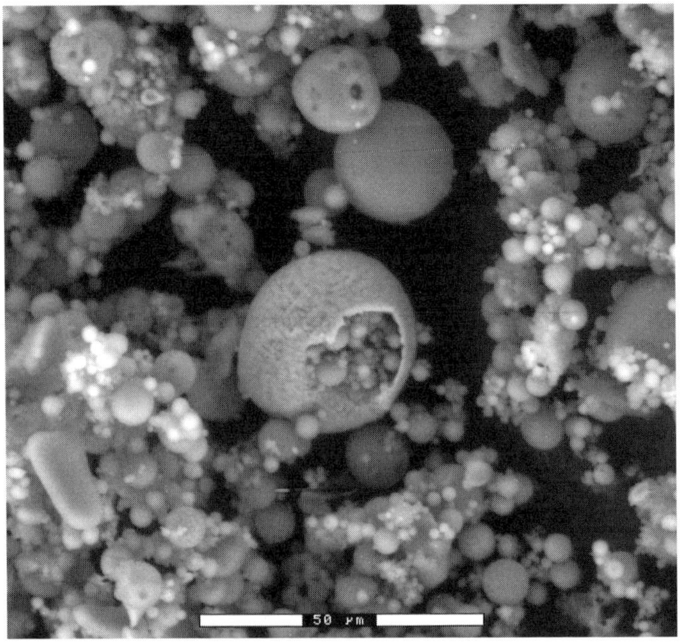

Figure C6 *Mortar structure for 1:3 NHL 3.5 lime with fly ash showing reaction at the fly ash particle surface.*

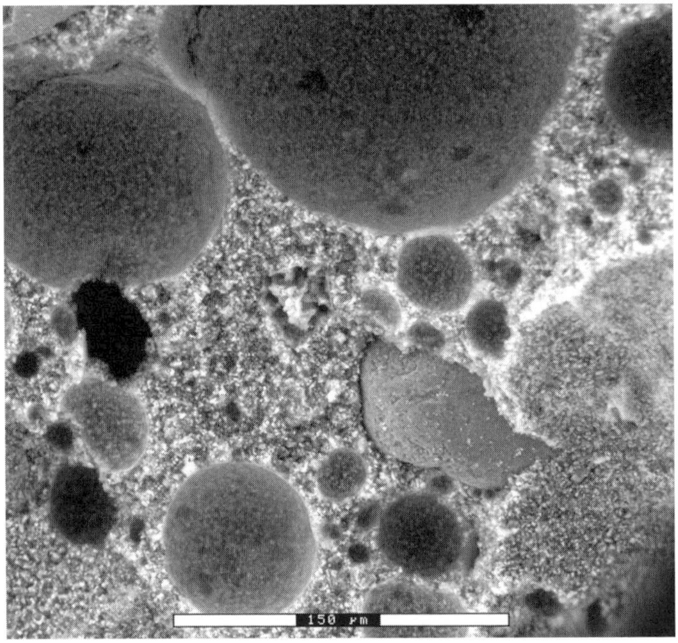

Figure C7 *Mortar structure for 1:3 NHL 3.5 lime with air-entraining admixture creating air bubbles.*